Hebrew Melodies

Hebrew Melodies

HEINRICH HEINE

Illustrated by
Mark Podwal

Translated by
Stephen Mitchell
and by Jack Prelutsky

With a foreword by
Elisheva Carlebach

The Pennsylvania
State University Press
University Park,
Pennsylvania

Library of Congress Cataloging-in-Publication Data

Names: Heine, Heinrich, 1797–1856, author. | Podwal, Mark
    H., 1945– illustrator. | Mitchell, Stephen, 1943– translator.
    | Prelutsky, Jack, translator. | Carlebach, Elisheva, writer of
    foreword. | Heine, Heinrich, 1797–1856. Hebräische Melodien. |
    Heine, Heinrich, 1797–1856. Hebräische Melodien. English.
Title: Hebrew melodies / Heinrich Heine ; illustrated by Mark
    Podwal ; translated by Stephen Mitchell and Jack Prelutsky ;
    with a foreword by Elisheva Carlebach.
Other titles: Dimyonot (University Park, Pa.)
Description: University Park, Pennsylvania : The Pennsylvania
    State University Press, [2019] | Series: Dimyonot: Jews and the
    cultural imagination | "The German text of Hebrew Melodies
    used in this volume derives from the Düsseldorf Heine Edition
    of Hebräische Melodien, edited by Frauke Bartelt and Alberto
    Destro (Hamburg: Hoffmann und Campe, 1992)"—Title page
    verso. | Includes bibliographical references and index. | Parallel
    English and German text; translated from German.
Summary: "A collection of poetry by 19th-century author Heinrich
    Heine, focusing on a return to a preoccupation with his Jewish
    roots, with new English translations alongside the original
    German"—Provided by publisher.
Identifiers: LCCN 2019024782 | ISBN 9780271084800 (cloth)
Subjects: LCGFT: Poetry.
Classification: LCC PT2316.H4 M55 2019 | DDC 892.4/14—dc2 3
LC record available at https://lccn.loc.gov/2019024782

Published by The Pennsylvania
State University Press,
University Park, PA 16802-1003

The Pennsylvania State University Press is a member of the
Association of University Presses.

It is the policy of The Pennsylvania State University Press to use
acid-free paper. Publications on uncoated stock satisfy the mini-
mum requirements of American National Standard for Information
Sciences—Permanence of Paper for Printed Library Material,
ANSI z39.48–1992.

The German text of *Hebrew Melodies* used in this volume derives
from the Düsseldorf Heine Edition of *Hebräische Melodien*, edited
by Frauke Bartelt and Alberto Destro (Hamburg: Hoffmann und
Campe, 1992).

In memory of my uncle

Julius Applebaum,

who introduced me

to Heine's *Disputation.*

—MARK PODWAL

Contents

Foreword

ELISHEVA CARLEBACH

A new English translation of Heinrich Heine's *Hebrew Melodies* is long overdue. Far more than freshly minted lines of verse, this volume contains an additional form of interpretive translation: Mark Podwal's inimitable artwork precisely captures the playful spirit and sweet comforts of Jewish tradition and the menacing edges of history's nightmares that characterize Heine's late-in-life return to his youthful memories. Distilling the spirit of Heine in any medium is no simple task. If ever a poet was caught between worlds, never quite at home in any of them, Heine stands as their model and bard. The great tensions of early nineteenth-century Europe coursed through his life—Germany or France, commerce or art, religion or rationalism, Jewishness or Christianity, acceptance or rejection—each a grand theme in its own right, and all of them subjects of his relentless pen.

Heine was born in 1797 in Düsseldorf, a city on Germany's riverine artery, the Rhine, during the time when it was under French occupation. He came of age at the height of what historians called a *Taufepidemie*, an epidemic of baptism that engulfed Germany's Jews in the early nineteenth century. For centuries Jews living in German lands had managed to cling to their tradition, to create and practice a distinctive culture in the face of cruelty and uncertainty that awaited them at every turn. There had always been a small number who despaired of a Jewish future and succumbed to the blandishments of Christian society. As with the Jewish converts of medieval Spain, the most articulate ones were placed in positions of prominence and tasked with persuading their Jewish brethren to follow them into baptism. The numbers of converts grew steadily, reaching a high point in the second decade of the nineteenth century. Many of the converts left writings about the Jewish lives of their youth or the circumstances of their conversion. In letters, diaries, ethnographies, and essays they poured out their hopes and disappointments, memories, theologies, and justifications. By the nineteenth century many urban, educated Jews came to believe that European culture was denominated Christian, that to enter it fully they had to abandon their Jewish particularism. Of all the very significant figures within the ranks of the converted, including Mendelssohns and Marxes, none rose to the literary fame of Heine, whose combined oeuvre of travel writing, political commentary, and lyric poetry vaulted him into the highest ranks of German poets and writers.

Heine began his education in traditional Jewish fashion under the tutelage of a *melammed* (traditional Jewish schoolmaster). It did not last long. His Jewish home life was bifurcated between a mother who disdained religious life and a father who favored it somewhat more. Attending Catholic schools, then university and law school, Heine joined an academic society of Jewish scholars that had been formed in the wake of the 1819 riots against Jews. This society, too, was short lived, but it had a profound impact. By reviving interest in the German Jewish past, it introduced Heine to medieval Jewish history and its sources. His re-creations of the Jewish past, while completely fanciful in their details, were in their main outlines rooted in his memories of childhood as well as in these brief excursions into Jewish tradition and history.

After a period of deliberation, Heine was baptized in a Lutheran church in 1825. "Baptized, but not converted," he wrote with bitterness about the exchange offered to young Jews, a "ticket" to a career in exchange for the religion of their ancestors. The official Jewish community resented these turncoats, and German society regarded them with suspicion. No academic or professional career materialized for Heine; perhaps in his heart of hearts he felt relieved, as this freed him to focus on his writing. While his *Buch der Lieder* (1827) proved to be immensely popular, Heine's liberal writings made him persona non grata in Germany, and by 1831 he had moved to Paris. From this perch in exile, Heine produced a prodigious body of work. His cultural criticism of bourgeois German pieties delighted enlightened readers and infuriated German officials. Heine reacted in incredulous fury when in 1840 the Jews of Damascus were

falsely accused of "devouring ancient monks" for religious reasons. Even young children were imprisoned and tortured over this ritual murder libel, yet the French consul and prime minister supported the charges. The incident moved him to return to a novel he had begun years earlier, one set in the Middle Ages with a ritual murder charge against a Jew at the center. *The Rabbi of Bacherach* was published as an incomplete novel; it was one of just a few writings he devoted to Jewish themes before *Hebrew Melodies*.

Hebrew Melodies

In the late 1840s, in physical agony and believing himself close to the end, Heine drew back from his usual political engagement and produced a masterly cycle of poems, *Romanzero* (1851). It consisted of three parts: *Histories*, *Lamentations*, and *Hebrew Melodies*. Like *Lamentations*, *Hebrew Melodies* signals Heine's preoccupation with ultimate things, among them the fate of his people. Heine once declared to a friend, "I make no secret of my Judaism, to which I have not returned, because I never left it."[1] This is not to say that Heine ever returned to any form of religious practice or belief. He admired the Jewish people for its gift of ethical consciousness and felt connected to it, but the undertone of mockery never quite disappeared from anything he wrote about it. Heine appropriated the title (but not the contents) of *Hebrew Melodies* from a collection of poems by Lord Byron, one of his favorite writers. Byron's turn to Jewish themes met with criticism and puzzlement in England, demonstrating that any sympathetic artist's attempt to elevate the plight of Jews—regardless of the writer's previous reputation—would meet with public scorn.

Hebrew Melodies itself consists of three separate, yet linked, poems: *Princess Sabbath* (*Prinzessin Sabbat*), *Yehuda ben Halévi*, and *Disputation*.[2] Trying to say what a poem is "about" is always an exercise in futility. Poems are about words, about metaphors, about close readings, and about elusive feelings. Heine's poems are dense with allusion, steeped in nostalgia, and edged in irony. Brahms, Mendelssohn, Schubert, and Schumann composed music inspired by Heine's poems; Mark Podwal's is the first modern attempt to capture their spirit in images. In the brief remarks that follow, I will not attempt to summarize the poems; they are here for the reader to savor in their unique flavor and glory. Instead I will choose a few thematic strands that stood out for me.

Princess Sabbath takes the dreary and abject existence of Jews—transformed into dogs in the eyes of the Christian world, "jeered and spat at" until they nearly became what their tormentors believed, "filled with doggish thoughts and instincts"—and contrasts that with the miraculous change wrought by the Sabbath, restoring dignity and joy to their inner life in synagogue and home. Heine's ode to the otherworldly spirit of the Sabbath lifts the veil from the public perception of Jews as dirty, debased, and grasping; within the serenity of their homes and rituals, they were as exalted as any nobility. The

Sabbath represented a flash of transcendence in the world of the mundane, the first of many divisions, contrasts, and paradoxes throughout the *Melodies*. *Yehuda ben Halévi*, whose protagonist no doubt reflected Heine's sensibility most closely, is filled with contrasting pairs. He recalls the square Hebrew letters of the Torah "from the very / Childhood of our world" and contrasts them with the Aramaic of the Targum—the former exalted, the latter akin to coarse dialect. Within the Talmud, he contrasts *halakha*, a school of dialectic, with *aggada*, a lush and fantastical garden in whose dreamy thickets he loses himself. *Disputation* is entirely a poem of contrast between the representatives of the dueling religions: the Christian, triumphalist and enraged, versus the Jew, rationalist and calm, each with a different conception of God, each absolutely certain of victory. It recalls the tenor of a famous disputation in thirteenth-century Barcelona, the last in which the Jewish representative was permitted to respond freely. The high stakes and supposed seriousness of the subject is abruptly reversed by the dismissive pronouncement of the bored queen. The two sides of the contest represent, in some fashion, the two sides of Heine's own riven life, and the conclusion represents his scornful judgment of the dogmatism of both institutional religions.

Exile is another motif that runs as a red thread through the entire set. An expatriate from Germany for most of his creative life, alienated from both the Jewish and Christian traditions, and removed from active life in his later years, Heine identified strongly with the plight of Jews as a people disembodied and dispersed. The quintessential exiles' lament, epitomized in the Psalm "By the Rivers of Babylon," has "seethed inside me . . . a thousand years already." *Hebrew Melodies* can be read, in its entirety, as Heine's response to the lament of the first Jewish exiles: "How can we sing God's song on alien soil?" *Yehuda ben Halévi* opens with that Psalm's immortal words of longing, "If I ever should forget thee, O Jerusalem." Heine's nostalgia and regret for the Jewish past he had spurned comes through in the many "insider" references to Jewish life. From the sublime tunes greeting the Sabbath to its ambrosial dishes and final sputtering taper, *Princess* revels in the senses that memories of Sabbath evoked. In *Yehuda* he recalled studying the Torah cantillation, the *tropp*, with its famous chain of trills, *shalshelet*. But perhaps nothing in the poem speaks as poignantly as his declaration that were he to ever come into possession of the casket containing the greatest treasures of Western civilization, "epics / Sung by the immortal Homer," *he* would have kept within it "All Yehuda ben Halévi's / Songs."

Hebrew Melodies allowed Heine to close a circle in his tormented life. But his visionary foreboding had a chilling afterlife. "If one day Satan . . . should be victorious, there will fall on the heads of the poor Jews a tempest of persecution, which will far surpass all their previous sufferings."[3] Engraved on the Berlin site of a 1933 Nazi book burning are Heine's prophetic words, "Where they burn books, they will also, in the end, burn people." Although the Nazis attempted to expunge all Jewish art from their culture and burned Heine's books, the popularity of his songs forced the Nazis to include them in anthologies, credited to "author unknown."

NOTES

1. Cited in Paul Mendes-Flohr and Jehuda Reinharz, eds., *The Jew in the Modern World: A Documentary History*, 2nd ed. (Oxford: Oxford University Press, 1995), 259.
2. The German texts of all three poems in *Hebrew Melodies* reproduced here are those of the Düsseldorfer Ausgabe.
3. Heinrich Heine, "Shakespeare's Maidens and Women," in *The Works of Heinrich Heine*, trans. Charles Leland (London: Heinemann, 1903), 1:400–401.

Acknowledgments

I would like to express my gratitude to the many who shared, encouraged, and supported my belief that a new illustrated translation of Heinrich Heine's *Hebrew Melodies* would be worth publishing.

For decades, ever since my uncle Julius Applebaum first introduced me to Heinrich Heine's poem *Disputation*, one of three poems that comprise *Hebrew Melodies*, I had wanted to illustrate its irreverent verses. Soon after the Berlin Jewish Museum included seven of my drawings in its golem exhibition, I reasoned that the museum would be an ideal venue to exhibit the illustrations I had in mind. Happily, the museum agreed and now owns the original art, which it will exhibit.

Not only have I enormously enjoyed creating the images for *Hebrew Melodies*, but I have been fortunate to collaborate with friends who are renowned in their fields. When I first proposed the project to Stephen Mitchell, his response was that because of many commitments, he could not begin a translation for at least a year. He soon wrote back, however, saying, "I have an earworm of Heine's rhythm sounding inside me," and within two or three months he had composed magnificent translations for *Princess Sabbath* and *Yehuda ben Halévi*. I am grateful also to Jack Prelutsky for his delightfully outrageous *Disputation* translation.

Professor Elisheva Carlebach has written an eloquent, poignant foreword, for which I am greatly indebted. I thank Professor Steven Fine for introducing the illustrations and translations to Penn State University Press director Patrick Alexander, who immediately agreed to publish this volume. I also thank Professor Samantha Baskind, editor of the Press's book series Dimyonot: Jews and the Cultural Imagination, for her enthusiasm for this publication. I am grateful for the heartfelt advice provided by Carol Kahn Strauss, former executive director of the Leo Baeck Institute, and Elisabeth Rochau-Shalem, senior editor at Hirmer Publishers. Finally, I deeply appreciate those who provided additional financial support, including The Plotkin Foundation, Joyce Berman, E. Jay Rosenstein, Michael Podwal, The Angelson Family Foundation, Gloria Pollack, Harvey and Dana Stone, and Hiram Hadad.

—MARK PODWAL

Hebrew Melodies

O laß nicht ohne Lebensgenuß

Dein Leben verfließen!

Und bist du sicher vor dem Schuß,

So laß sie nur schießen.

Fliegt dir das Glück vorbey einmahl,

So fass' es am Zipfel.

Auch rath' ich dir, baue dein Hüttchen im Thal

Und nicht auf dem Gipfel.

Don't let your life go by

without enjoying it.

And when you're safe from harm,

let them shoot as they please.

If happiness should pass by,

catch it by the tail.

Build your cabin in the valley,

not on the peak.

BECOMES A HUMAN ONCE AGAIN

Prinzessin Sabbath

In Arabiens Mährchenbuche
Sehen wir verwünschte Prinzen,
Die zu Zeiten ihre schöne
Urgestalt zurückgewinnen:

Das behaarte Ungeheuer
Ist ein Königsohn geworden;
Schmuckreich glänzend angekleidet,
Auch verliebt die Flöte blasend.

Doch die Zauberfrist zerrinnt,
Und wir schauen plötzlich wieder
Seine königliche Hoheit
In ein Ungethüm verzottelt.

Einen Prinzen solchen Schicksals
Singt mein Lied. Er ist geheißen
Israel. Ihn hat verwandelt
Hexenspruch in einen Hund.

Hund mit hündischen Gedanken,
Kötert er die ganze Woche
Durch des Lebens Koth und Kehricht,
Gassenbuben zum Gespötte.

Aber jeden Freytag Abend,
In der Dämmrungstunde, plötzlich
Weicht der Zauber, und der Hund
Wird aufs Neu' ein menschlich Wesen.

Princess Sabbath

In Arabia's book of legends
There are heroes who, bewitched once,
Have recovered from the spell
And regained their former beauty.

The grotesque, repulsive creature
Has become a prince again,
Richly clad in silks and jewels,
Serenading his belovèd.

Soon, though, the reprieve is over,
And we see His Royal Highness   10
Suddenly transmogrified
Back into a hairy monster.

Such a prince, with such a burden,
Is the subject of my song. His
Name is Israel. By some witch's
Spell he has become a dog.

Filled with doggish thoughts and instincts,
All week long he sniffs his way through
Life's assorted muck and rubbish,
Jeered and spat at by street urchins.   20

But each week, on Friday evening,
At the twilight hour, the deadly
Magic softens, and the dog be-
comes a human once again.

GREETINGS, O BELOVÈD MANSION OF THE LORD

Mensch mit menschlichen Gefühlen,
Mit erhobnem Haupt und Herzen,
Festlich, reinlich schier gekleidet,
Tritt er in des Vaters Halle.

»Sey gegrüßt, geliebte Halle
Meines königlichen Vaters!
Zelte Jakobs, Eure heil'gen
Eingangspfosten küßt mein Mund!«

Durch das Haus geheimnißvoll
Zieht ein Wispern und ein Weben,
Und der unsichtbare Hausherr
Athmet schaurig in der Stille.

Stille! Nur der Seneschall
(Vulgo Synagogendiener)
Springt geschäftig auf und nieder,
Um die Lampen anzuzünden.

Trostverheißend goldne Lichter,
Wie sie glänzen, wie sie glimmern!
Stolz aufflackern auch die Kerzen
Auf der Brüstung des Almemors.

Vor dem Schreine, der die Thora
Aufbewahret und verhängt ist
Mit der kostbar seidnen Decke,
Die von Edelsteinen funkelt—

Dort an seinem Betpultständer
Steht schon der Gemeindesänger;
Schmuckes Männchen, das sein schwarzes
Mäntelchen kokett geachselt.

Human now, with human feelings,
Dressed in pure and festive clothes, he
Stands before his Father's mansion
With uplifted head and heart.

"Greetings, O belovèd mansion
Of the Lord, my royal Father!   30
Tents of Jacob, with great fervor
I now kiss Your holy doorposts!"

Through the house mysteriously
Moves a whispering, a murmur,
And at once the unseen Master
Breathes, uncanny, in the silence.

Silence! Now the sacristan
(Beadle, to use common parlance)
Bustles up and down and sideways,
Lighting all the holy lampwicks.   40

These consoling candelabras,
How they glitter, how they sparkle!
Proudly, too, the candles flicker
On the *bimah*'s wooden railing.

Near the shrine in which the Torah
Lies protected, richly curtained
With a costly silken cover
Shimmering with precious gemstones,

At his little polished prayer desk
Stands the congregation's cantor;   50
Dapper little man, his black robe
Hangs demurely on his shoulders,

LIGHTING ALL THE HOLY LAMPWICKS

THE TORAH LIES PROTECTED, RICHLY CURTAINED

Um die weiße Hand zu zeigen,	And, to show how white his hand, he
Haspelt er am Halse, seltsam	Fidgets with his neck quite oddly,
An die Schläf' den Zeigefinger,	Index finger pressed to temple
An die Kehl' den Daumen drückend.	And his thumb against his throat.
Trällert vor sich hin ganz leise,	To himself he hums sedately,
Bis er endlich lautaufjubelnd	Till at last his voice, exulting,
Seine Stimm' erhebt und singt:	Bursts out in a joyful music:
Lecho Daudi Likras Kalle!	*"Lécho, dódi, líkras kálle!* 60
Lecho Daudi Likras Kalle—	*"Lécho, dódi, líkras kálle—*
Komm', Geliebter, deiner harret	Come, my dear, the Bride awaits you,
Schon die Braut, die dir entschleyert	Chaste and ready to uncover
Ihr verschämtes Angesicht!	To your eyes her blushing face!"
Dieses hübsche Hochzeitcarmen	A delightful wedding poem,
Ist gedichtet von dem großen,	Written by the great and very
Hochberühmten Minnesinger	Famous Jewish troubadour
Don Jehuda ben Halevy.	Don Yehuda ben Halévi.
In dem Liede wird gefeyert	In this song he celebrates
Die Vermählung Israels	Israel's wedding ceremony 70
Mit der Frau Prinzessin Sabbath,	With Her Highness Lady Sabbath,
Die man nennt die stille Fürstin.	Who is called "the silent princess."
Perl' und Blume aller Schönheit	Pearl and flower of all beauty
Ist die Fürstin. Schöner war	Is the princess. Not more lovely
Nicht die Königin von Saba,	Was the far-famed Queen of Sheba,
Salomonis Busenfreundin,	Bosom friend of Solomon,
Die, ein Blaustrumpf Aethiopiens,	Ethiopia's bluestocking,
Durch Esprit brilliren wollte,	Whose ambition was to dazzle
Und mit ihren klugen Räthseln	With her clever riddles but
Auf die Länge fatigant ward.	In the end became annoying. 80

ISRAEL'S WEDDING CEREMONY

Die Prinzessin Sabbath, welche
Ja die personifizierte
Ruhe ist, verabscheut alle
Geisteskämpfe und Debatten.

Gleich fatal ist ihr die trampelnd
Deklamirende Passion,
Jenes Pathos, das mit flatternd
Aufgelöstem Haar einherstürmt.

Sittsam birgt die stille Fürstin
In der Haube ihre Zöpfe;
Blickt so sanft wie die Gazelle,
Blüht so schlank wie eine Addas.

Sie erlaubt dem Liebsten alles,
Ausgenommen Tabakrauchen—
»Liebster! rauchen ist verboten,
Weil es heute Sabbath ist.

»Dafür aber heute Mittag
Soll dir dampfen, zum Ersatz,
Ein Gericht, das wahrhaft göttlich—
Heute sollst du Schalet essen!«

Schalet, schöner Götterfunken,
Tochter aus Elysium!
Also klänge Schillers Hochlied,
Hätt' er Schalet je gekostet.

Schalet ist die Himmelspeise,
Die der liebe Herrgott selber
Einst den Moses kochen lehrte
Auf dem Berge Sinai,

Princess Sabbath, who indeed is
The embodiment of stillness,
Hates and has contempt for such
Intellectual sparring matches.

Just as loathsome in her eyes is
Any ostentatious passion,
Pathos punctuated by the
Preacher's long locks, wildly shaken.

Modestly the silent princess
Hides her tresses in her bonnet,   90
Looks up softly with gazelle eyes,
Blossoms like the slender myrtle.

She allows her sweet belovèd
Everything—except tobacco.
"Dearest, smoking is forbidden,
Since today we keep the Sabbath.

"But at noon, in compensation,
You shall have a steaming bowl
Of a food divinely luscious—
You shall feast today on *cholent*!"   100

Cholent, light direct from heaven,
Daughter of Elysium!
Thus would Schiller's ode have sounded
Had he ever tasted *cholent*.

Cholent is the delicacy
That the Lord revealed to Moses,
Teaching him the way to cook it
On the summit of Mount Sinai,

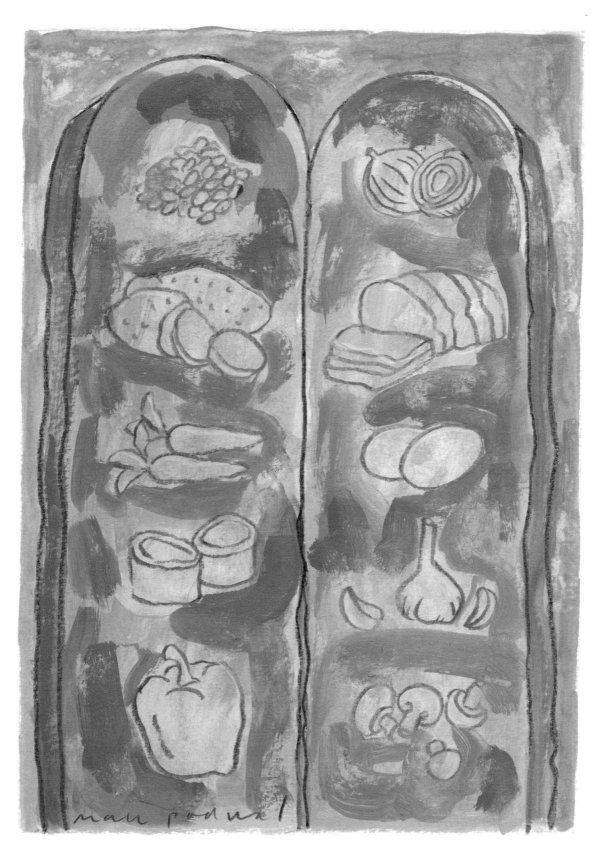

CHOLENT IS THE DELICACY THAT THE LORD REVEALED TO MOSES

CURSE'S EVIL HOUR

Wo der Allerhöchste gleichfalls	On the very spot where the All-
All die guten Glaubenslehren	High revealed His moral doctrines
Und die heil'gen zehn Gebote	And the holy Ten Commandments
Wetterleuchtend offenbarte.	In the midst of flames and lightning.

Wo der Allerhöchste gleichfalls
All die guten Glaubenslehren
Und die heil'gen zehn Gebote
Wetterleuchtend offenbarte.

On the very spot where the All-
High revealed His moral doctrines   110
And the holy Ten Commandments
In the midst of flames and lightning.

Schalet ist des wahren Gottes
Koscheres Ambrosia,
Wonnebrod des Paradieses,
Und mit solcher Kost verglichen

Cholent is God's strictly kosher
Certified and blessed ambrosia,
Manna meant for Paradise, and
So, compared with such an offering,

Ist nur eitel Teufelsdreck
Das Ambrosia der falschen
Heidengötter Griechenlands,
Die verkappte Teufel waren.

The ambrosia of the phony
Heathen gods of ancient Greece
(Who were devils in disguise) is
Just a pile of devils' droppings.   120

Speist der Prinz von solcher Speise,
Glänzt sein Auge wie verkläret,
Und er knöpfet auf die Weste,
Und er spricht mit sel'gem Lächeln:

Once the prince has tasted *cholent*,
He lights up, as if transfigured,
And unbuttoning his waistcoat
With a blissful smile he muses:

»Hör' ich nicht den Jordan rauschen?
Sind das nicht die Brüßelbrunnen
In dem Palmenthal von Beth-El,
Wo gelagert die Kamehle?

"Don't I hear the Jordan murmur?
Aren't these the flowing fountains
In the palmy Bethel valley
Where we have tied up our camels?

Hör' ich nicht die Heerdenglöckchen?
Sind das nicht die fetten Hämmel,
Die vom Gileath-Gebirge
Abendlich der Hirt herabtreibt?«

"Don't I hear the sheep-bells ringing?
Aren't these the fattened rams   130
That the shepherd in the twilight
Drives down from Mount Gilead?"

Doch der schöne Tage verflittert;
Wie mit langen Schattenbeinen
Kommt geschritten der Verwünschung
Böse Stund'—Es seufzt der Prinz.

But the lovely day is flying
Off, and with long shadow-legs the
Curse's evil hour strides toward him,
And the prince lets out a sigh,

SPICE BOX

Ist ihm doch als griffen eiskalt
Hexenfinger in sein Herze.
Schon durchrieseln ihn die Schauer
Hündischer Metamorphose.

Die Prinzessin reicht dem Prinzen
Ihre güldne Nardenbüchse.
Langsam riecht er—Will sich laben
Noch einmal an Wohlgerüchen.

Es kredenzet die Prinzessin
Auch den Abschiedstrunk dem Prinzen—
Hastig trinkt er, und im Becher
Bleiben wen'ge Tropfen nur.

Er besprengt damit den Tisch,
Nimmt alsdann ein kleines Wachslicht,
Und er tunkt es in die Nässe,
Daß es knistert und erlischt.

Seems to feel the icy fingers
Of a witch around his heart,
Shudders at the fast approaching
Doggish metamorphosis.   140

Princess Sabbath hands her golden
Spice box to the prince. Inhaling
Deeply, he luxuriates
In its fragrance one last time.

Then the princess offers him the
Drink of parting, and he drinks it
Quickly; in the silver goblet
Just a few last drops remain.

These he sprinkles on the table.
Then he takes a small wax taper,   150
And he dips it in the moisture
Till it sputters and goes out.

—TRANSLATED BY STEPHEN MITCHELL

"IF I EVER SHOULD FORGET THEE, O JERUSALEM"

Jehuda ben Halevy

Yehuda ben Halévi

I

»Lechzend klebe mir die Zunge
An dem Gaumen, und es welke
Meine rechte Hand, vergäß ich
Jemals dein, Jerusalem—«

Wort und Weise, unaufhörlich
Schwirren sie mir heut' im Kopfe,
Und mir ist als hört' ich Stimmen,
Psalmodirend, Männerstimmen—

Manchmal kommen auch zur Vorschein
Bärte, schattig lange Bärte—
Traumgestalten, wer von euch
Ist Jehuda ben Halevy?

Doch sie huschen rasch vorüber;
Die Gespenster scheuen furchtsam
Der Lebend'gen plumpen Zuspruch—
Aber ihn hab' ich erkannt—

Ich erkannt' ihn an der bleichen
Und gedankenstolzen Stirne,
An der Augen süßer Starrheit—
Sahn mich an so schmerzlich forschend—

Doch zumeist erkannt ich ihn
An dem räthselhaften Lächeln
Jener schön gereimten Lippen,
Die man nur bey Dichtern findet.

I

"If I ever should forget thee,
O Jerusalem, let my right hand
Lose its cunning, let my tongue
Cleave forever to my palate—"

Words and music, without ceasing,
Swirl inside my head today, and
Now I seem to hear men's voices,
Ancient voices, chanting psalms;

Sometimes I can catch a glimpse of
Beards—of long beards wreathed in shadows.   10
Tell me, dream forms, which of you
Is Yehuda ben Halévi?

But they quickly hurry past me—
Ghosts will always shun the awkward
Consolations of the living—
Yet, in spite of that, I knew him—

Knew him by his noble forehead,
Pale and filled with lofty thoughts—
And his piercing eyes gazed deeply
Into mine, with boundless sorrow.   20

First and foremost, though, I knew him
By the smile, so enigmatic,
On those beautiful rhymed lips
That one finds with poets only.

Jahre kommen und verfließen.
Seit Jehuda ben Halevy
Ward geboren, sind verflossen
Sieben hundert fünfzig Jahre—

Hat zuerst das Licht erblickt
Zu Toledo in Castilien,
Und es hat der goldne Tajo
Ihm sein Wiegenlied gelullet.

Für Entwicklung seines Geistes
Sorgte früh der strenge Vater,
Der den Unterricht begann
Mit dem Gottesbuch, der Thora.

Diese las er mit dem Sohne
In dem Urtext, dessen schöne,
Hieroglyphisch pittoreske,
Altcaldäische Quadratschrift

Herstammt aus dem Kindesalter
Unsrer Welt, und auch deswegen
Jedem kindlichen Gemüthe
So vertraut entgegenlacht.

Diesen echten alten Text
Rezitirte auch der Knabe
In der uralt hergebrachten
Singsang-Weise, Tropp geheißen—

Und er gurgelte gar lieblich
Jene fetten Gutturalen,
Und er schlug dabey den Triller,
Den Schalscheleth, wie ein Vogel.

Years keep coming and dissolving.
It is seven hundred fifty
Years already since the birth
Of Yehuda ben Halévi.

His birth city was Toledo
In the kingdom of Castile;   30
With its lullabies the golden
Tagus soothed him in his cradle.

His young mind's development
Was advanced by his stern father,
Who began his education
With the Holy Book, the Torah.

With his little son he read it
In the Hebrew text, whose lovely
Hieroglyphically graceful
Old Chaldean square-script letters   40

Have descended from the very
Childhood of our world and therefore
Seem to intimately smile upon
Anyone whose mind is childlike.

This authentic, ancient text the
Boy recited in the singsong
Measure, called the *trope* in Yiddish,
Passed down from primeval ages.

And he gurgled very sweetly
All those juicy gutturals,   50
And he trilled the cantillation
Of *shalshélet* like a bird.

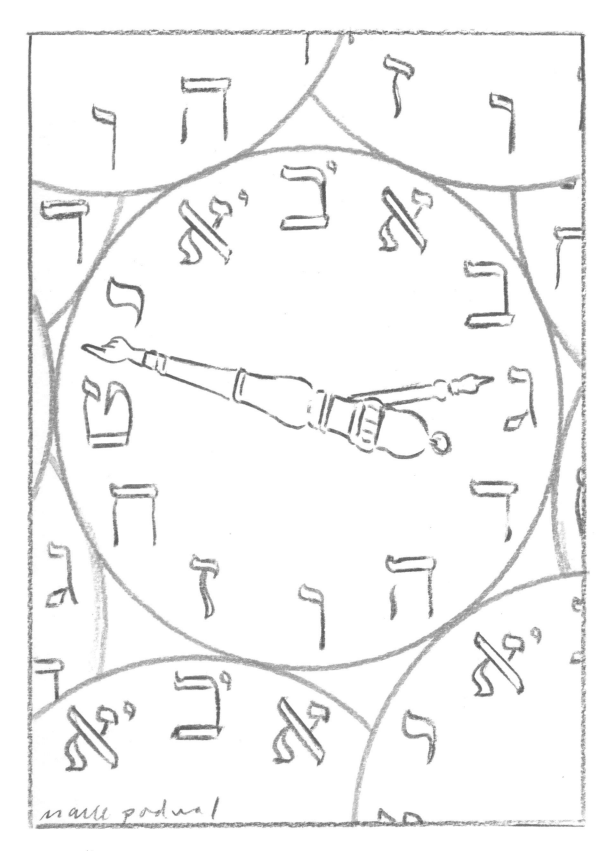

YEARS KEEP COMING AND DISSOLVING

HIS STERN FATHER, WHO BEGAN HIS EDUCATION WITH THE HOLY BOOK, THE TORAH

AND HE TRILLED THE CANTILLATION OF *SHALSHÉLET* LIKE A BIRD

Auch den Targum Onkelos,	And the Targum Onkelos—
Der geschrieben ist in jenem	Which was written in the curious
Plattjudäischen Idiom,	Antique Jewish dialect
Das wir aramäisch nennen	That is known as Aramaic
Und zur Sprache der Propheten	And that has the same relation
Sich verhalten mag etwa	To the language of the prophets
Wie das Schwäbische zum Deutschen—	That our Swabian has to German—
Dieses Gelbveiglein-Hebräisch	This eccentric homespun Hebrew
Lernte gleichfalls früh der Knabe,	He learned also, very early,
Und es kam ihm solche Kenntniß	And the knowledge came in handy
Bald darauf sehr gut zu Statten	When the boy began his long and
Bey dem Studium des Talmuds.	Patient study of the Talmud.
Ja, frühzeitig hat der Vater	Yes, his father early led him
Ihn geleitet zu dem Talmud,	To the pages of the Talmud,
Und da hat er ihm erschlossen	And he introduced him to
Die Halacha, diese große	The *halákha*, that tremendous
Fechterschule, wo die besten	School of fencing, where the greatest
Dialektischen Athleten	Of the dialectic athletes
Babylons und Pumpedithas	In the town of Pumbedita
Ihre Kämpferspiele trieben.	Did their intellectual jousting.
Lernen konnte hier der Knabe	Here the boy began to study
Alle Künste der Polemik;	Strict polemics, and he later
Seine Meisterschaft bezeugte	Showed his mastery of the subject
Späterhin das Buch Cosari.	In his Book of the Kuzari.
Doch der Himmel gießt herunter	But the heavens pour upon us
Zwey verschiedne Sorten Lichtes:	Two quite different kinds of brightness—
Grelles Tageslicht der Sonne	The harsh daylight of the sun
Und das mildre Mondlicht—Also,	And the milder moonlight—so the

Line numbers: 60, 70, 80

Also leuchtet auch der Talmud	Talmud also has two kinds of
Zwiefach, und man theilt ihn ein	Light, and it is thus partitioned
In Halacha und Hagada.	In *halákha* and *aggádah*.
Erstre nannt' ich eine Fechtschul'—	Fencing school I called the former,
Letztre aber, die Hagada,	But the latter, the *aggádah*,
Will ich einen Garten nennen,	I would rather call a garden,
Einen Garten, hochphantastisch	Planted with the strangest, most fan-
Und vergleichbar jenem andern,	tastical of flowers, like that
Welcher ebenfalls dem Boden	Other garden that once sprouted
Babylons entsprossen weiland—	From the soil of Babylon: the
Garten der Semiramis,	Garden of Semíramis,
Achtes Wunderwerk der Welt.	The eighth wonder of the world.
Königin Semiramis,	This great queen, Semíramis,
Die als Kind erzogen worden	Who was found and raised by birds
Von den Vögeln, und gar manche	And retained, as she grew older,
Vögelthümlichkeit bewahrte,	Many birdlike traits and habits,
Wollte nicht auf platter Erde	Didn't like to go out walking
Promeniren wie wir andern	On the ground, like all us other
Säugethiere, und sie pflanzte	Mammals, so she had her servants
Einen Garten in der Luft—	Plant a garden in the air—
Hoch auf kolossalen Säulen	High up on colossal pillars
Prangten Palmen und Cypressen,	Cypresses and palm trees flourished,
Goldorangen, Blumenbeete,	Flower beds, wisteria,
Marmorbilder, auch Springbrunnen,	Marble statues, fountains also,
Alles klug und fest verbunden	The whole garden cunningly
Durch unzähl'ge Hänge-Brücken,	Joined by countless hanging bridges
Die wie Schlingepflanzen aussahn	Made to look like vines and creepers
Und worauf sich Vögel wiegten—	And upon which birds stood, swaying—

90

100

THIS GREAT QUEEN, SEMÍRAMIS, WHO WAS FOUND AND RAISED BY BIRDS

Große, bunte, ernste Vögel,
Tiefe Denker, die nicht singen,
Während sie umflattert kleines
Zeisigvolk, das lustig trillert—

Alle athmen ein, beseligt,
Einen reinen Balsamduft,
Welcher unvermischt mit schnödem
Erdendunst und Mißgeruche.

Die Hagada ist ein Garten
Solcher Luftkindgrillen-Art,
Und der junge Talmudschüler,
Wenn sein Herze war bestäubet

Und betäubet vom Gezänke
Der Halacha, vom Dispute
Ueber das fatale Ey,
Das ein Huhn gelegt am Festtag,

Oder über eine Frage
Gleicher Importanz—der Knabe
Floh alsdann sich zu erfrischen
In die blühende Hagada,

Wo die schönen alten Sagen,
Engelmährchen und Legenden,
Stille Märtyrerhistorien,
Festgesänge, Weisheitsprüche,

Auch Hyperbeln, gar possirlich,
Alles aber glaubenskräftig,
Glaubensglühend—O, das glänzte,
Quoll und sproß so überschwenglich—

Large, bright-colored birds, deep thinkers
Who were too absorbed to sing, while   110
All around them fluttered flocks of
Little finches, warbling gaily—

All of them elated, breathing
Such pure air, a balmy fragrance,
Unpolluted by the squalid
Odors of the earth beneath them.

The *aggádah* is a garden
Made of such celestial whimsy,
And the young Talmudic scholar,
When his heart was stupefied   120

By the constant bickering
He would find in the *halákha*,
With disputes about the awkward
Egg the hen laid on a feast day,

Or about some other question
Equally profound—the boy
Fled that part to seek refreshment
In the blossoming *aggádah*,

Where the beautiful old tales were,
Tales of angels, myths and legends,   130
Tranquil stories of the martyrs,
Hymns and epigrams and proverbs,

Comical exaggerations—
Yet these pages glowed with such great
Faith and passion, oh they shimmered,
Glowed with such exuberance—

THE AGGÁDAH IS A GARDEN

Und des Knaben edles Herze	And the young boy's noble heart was
Ward ergriffen von der wilden,	Captivated by the wild
Abentheuerlichen Süße,	Sweetness, by the fearless daring,
Von der wundersamen Schmerzlust	By the wondrous aching rapture 140
Und den fabelhaften Schauern	And by the amazing shudders
Jener seligen Geheimwelt,	Of that blissful secret world,
Jener großen Offenbarung,	Of that mighty revelation
Die wir nennen Poesie.	Known to us as poetry.
Auch die Kunst der Poesie,	And the craft that makes it happen—
Heitres Wissen, holdes Können,	Cheerful knowledge, lovely power,
Welches wir die Dichtkunst heißen,	That we call the poet's art—
That sich auf dem Sinn des Knaben.	Deepened in his understanding.
Und Jehuda ben Halevy	Thus Yehuda ben Halévi
Ward nicht bloß ein Schriftgelehrter,	Grew to be not just a scholar 150
Sondern auch der Dichtkunst Meister,	But a master of his language
Sondern auch ein großer Dichter.	And a great and mighty poet.
Ja, er ward ein großer Dichter,	Yes, he was a mighty poet,
Stern und Fackel seiner Zeit,	Star and beacon for his people
Seines Volkes Licht und Leuchte,	And the light of that whole era,
Eine wunderbare, große	An immense and wonderful
Feuersäule des Gesanges,	Pillar of poetic fire
Die der Schmerzenskarawane	Moving out in front of Israel's
Israels vorangezogen	Caravan of grief and anguish
In der Wüste des Exils.	In the wilderness of exile. 160
Rein und wahrhaft, sonder Makel	Pure and truthful, without blemish,
War sein Lied, wie seine Seele—	Were his poems, like his soul.
Als der Schöpfer sie erschaffen,	The Creator, when He made it,
Diese Seele, selbstzufrieden	Very pleased with His creation,

Küßte er die schöne Seele,
Und des Kusses holder Nachklang
Bebt in jedem Lied des Dichters,
Das geweiht durch diese Gnade.

Wie im Leben, so im Dichten
Ist das höchste Gut die Gnade—
Wer sie hat, der kann nicht sünd'gen
Nicht in Versen, noch in Prosa.

Solchen Dichter von der Gnade
Gottes nennen wir Genie:
Unverantwortlicher König
Des Gedankenreiches ist er.

Nur dem Gotte steht er Rede,
Nicht dem Volke—In der Kunst,
Wie im Leben, kann das Volk
Töten uns, doch niemals richten.—

II

Bey den Wassern Babels saßen
Wir und weinten, unsre Harfen
Lehnten an den Trauerweiden—
Kennst du noch das alte Lied?

Kennst du noch die alte Weise,
Die im Anfang so elegisch
Greint und sumset, wie ein Kessel,
Welcher auf dem Herde kocht?

Lange schon, jahrtausendlange
Kocht's in mir. Ein dunkles Wehe!
Und die Zeit leckt meine Wunde,
Wie der Hund die Schwären Hiobs.

Kissed that lovely soul; the echo
Of His kiss kept resonating
Through the poet's lovely verses,
Consecrated by this grace.

As in life, in poems also,
Grace is the surpassing virtue—   170
He who has it can commit no
Sin in either verse or prose.

Any poet open to the
Grace of God we call a genius:
Monarch in the realm of thought and
Free of any human critics,

Answerable to God alone,
Not the public. For in art,
As in life, the public can just
Kill us, but they cannot judge us.   180

II

"By the streams of Babylon
We sat down and wept for Zion,
Hung our harps upon the willows."
That old song—do you still know it?

Do you know the ancient lyric
That begins with such lamenting,
Groans and hisses like a kettle
Boiling over on the hearth?

Long—a thousand years already—
This dark woe has seethed inside me.   190
And Time comes and licks my wounds
Like the dog that licked Job's pustules.

THAT OLD SONG—DO YOU STILL KNOW IT?

AND MY PRECIOUS WINGÈD HORSE

Dank dir, Hund, für deinen Speichel—	Dog, I thank you for your spittle,
Doch das kann nur kühlend lindern—	But it merely cools and soothes—
Heilen kann mich nur der Tod,	Only death can come and heal me,
Aber, ach, ich bin unsterblich!	But, alas, I am immortal!
Jahre kommen und vergehen—	Years keep coming and dissolving—
In dem Webstuhl läuft geschäftig	In the loom the spool keeps whirring
Schnurrend hin und her die Spule—	As it races to and fro, and
Was er webt, das weiß kein Weber.	What it weaves, no weaver knows.
Jahre kommen und vergehen,	Years keep coming and dissolving,
Menschenthränen träufeln, rinnen	And men's teardrops trickle slowly
Auf die Erde, und die Erde	Downward to the earth, and earth just
Saugt sie ein mit stiller Gier—	Sucks them in with silent greed—
Tolle Sud! Der Deckel springt—	Seething rage! The lid blows off now—
Heil dem Manne, dessen Hand	"Happy shall he be who pays you
Deine junge Brut ergreifet	Back, who takes your little ones and
Und zerschmettert an der Felswand.	Dashes them against the rocks."
Gott sey Dank! die Sud verdampfet	Thanks to God, the boiling stops, the
In dem Kessel, der allmählig	Kettle cools, and gradually
Ganz verstummt. Es weicht mein Spleen,	Silence reigns. Now my dejection
Mein westöstlich dunkler Spleen—	Eases, my dark Jewish gloom—
Auch mein Flügelrößlein wiehert	And my precious wingèd horse now
Wieder heiter, scheint den bösen	Whinnies cheerfully and seems to
Nachtalp von sich abzuschütteln,	Shake off this whole horrid nightmare,
Und die klugen Augen fragen:	Looks at me and seems to ask:
Reiten wir zurück nach Spanien	"Shouldn't we go back to Spain now,
Zu dem kleinen Talmudisten,	To the little Talmud scholar
Der ein großer Dichter worden,	Who became a mighty poet—
Zu Jehuda ben Halevy?	To Yehuda ben Halévi?"

Line numbers: 200, 210, 220

Ja, er ward ein großer Dichter,
Absoluter Traumweltsherrscher
Mit der Geisterkönigskrone,
Ein Poet von Gottes Gnade,

Der in heiligen Sirventen,
Madrigalen und Terzinen,
Canzonetten und Ghaselen
Ausgegossen alle Flammen

Seiner gottgeküßten Seele!
Wahrlich ebenbürtig war
Dieser Troubadour den besten
Lautenschlägern der Provence,

Poitous und der Guienne,
Roussillons und aller andern
Süßen Pomeranzenlande
Der galanten Christenheit.

Der galanten Christenheit
Süße Pomeranzenlande!
Wie sie duften, glänzen, klingen
In dem Zwielicht der Erinnrung!

Schöne Nachtigallenwelt!
Wo man statt des wahren Gottes
Nur den falschen Gott der Liebe
Und der Musen angebeten.

Clerici mit Rosenkränzen
Auf der Glatze, sangen Psalmen
In der heitern Sprache *d'oc*;
Und die Layen, edle Ritter,

Yes, he was a mighty poet,
Ruler of a world of dream forms,
Monarch of the spirit realm—a
Poet by the grace of Heaven,

Who in his devout sirventes,
Madrigals and pastorales,
Canzonets, ghazals, ballatas,
Poured out all the fiery passions

Of his God-kissed poet's soul.
Yes, this troubadour was equal   230
To the greatest of the poet-
Lutenists in all Provence,

Poitou, Roussillon, Guyenne,
Languedoc, and all the other
Sweet lands where the orange blossoms
Grow in gallant Christendom.

Lands of gallant Christendom,
Where the orange blossoms flourish!
How they smell and sound and glisten
In the twilight of remembrance!   240

World of nightingales, how lovely!
Where instead of the true God
Just the false god of erotic love was
Worshipped, and the Muses also.

Clergymen with wreaths of roses
On their shining pates sang hymns
In their cheerful Provençal;
And the noble knights and barons,

Stolz auf hohen Rossen trabend,	Trotting on their purebred horses,
Spintisirten Vers und Reime	Meditated on the verses 250
Zur Verherrlichung der Dame,	That would glorify the ladies
Der ihr Herze fröhlich diente.	Whom their hearts so gladly served.
Ohne Dame keine Minne,	If no lady, then no love—so
Und es war dem Minnesänger	To the troubadour, a lady
Unentbehrlich eine Dame,	Was as indispensable as
Wie dem Butterbrot die Butter.	Butter is to buttered bread.
Auch der Held, den wir besingen,	Well, the hero whom I sing of,
Auch Jehuda ben Halevy	Don Yehuda ben Halévi,
Hatte seine Herzensdame;	Also worshipped his belovèd,
Doch sie war besondrer Art.	But she was a special instance. 260
Sie war keine Laura, deren	For this lady was no Laura,
Augen, sterbliche Gestirne,	Whose bright eyes, like mortal stars,
In dem Dome am Charfreytag	In the Duomo on Good Friday
Den berühmten Brand gestiftet—	Set a poet's heart on fire—
Sie war keine Chatelaine,	Nor a lovely noblewoman
Die im Blüthenschmuck der Jugend	In the flower of youth, presiding
Bey Turniren präsidirte	Over a great tournament and
Und den Lorbeerkranz ertheilte—	Placing laurel wreaths on winners—
Keine Kußrechtscasuistin	Nor was she a learnèd jurist
War sie, keine Doktrinärrin,	In the Court of Love, who lectured 270
Die im Spruchcollegium	On the laws concerning kisses,
Eines Minnehofs dozirte—	When and where they were allowed.
Jene, die der Rabbi liebte,	She, the one the rabbi longed for,
War ein traurig armes Liebchen,	Was a poor, heart-shattered lady,
Der Zerstörung Jammerbildniß,	Mournful victim of destruction,
Und sie hieß Jerusalem.	And was named Jerusalem.

Schon in frühen Kindestagen	Even in his early childhood
War sie seine ganze Liebe;	All his love was pledged to her,
Sein Gemüthe machte beben	And his soul already quivered
Schon das Wort Jerusalem.	At the word *Jerusalem*. 280
Purpurflamme auf der Wange,	Then the boy stood rapt and listened,
Stand der Knabe, und er horchte,	Cheeks and forehead flaming scarlet,
Wenn ein Pilger nach Toledo	When a pilgrim journeyed from the
Kam aus fernem Morgenlande	Holy Land and reached Toledo,
Und erzählte: wie verödet	And described how devastated
Und verunreint jetzt die Stätte,	And polluted was the city—
Wo am Boden noch die Lichtspur	Though a trail of light still lingered
Von dem Fuße der Propheten—	From the footsteps of the prophets,
Wo die Luft noch balsamiret	And the air was still perfumed with
Von dem ew'gen Odem Gottes—	The eternal breath of God. 290
O des Jammeranblicks! rief	"Such a bitter desolation!"
Einst ein Pilger, dessen Bart	Cried the pilgrim, whose white-silver
Silberweiß hinabfloß, während	Beard flowed down below his waist, and
Sich das Barthaar an der Spitze	As it reached its tip, the beard-hair
Wieder schwärzte und es aussah,	Darkened, and it looked as if the
Als ob sich der Bart verjünge—	Beard had all at once grown younger.
Ein gar wunderlicher Pilger	Such an interesting, strange pilgrim
Mocht' es seyn, die Augen lugten	Must the man have been; his eyes
Wie aus tausendjähr'gem Trübsinn,	Peered out from a thousand years of
Und er seufzt': »Jerusalem!	Gloom. He sighed, "Jerusalem, 300
Sie, die volkreich heil'ge Stadt	"Once a crowded holy city,
Ist zur Wüsteney geworden,	Has become a wilderness
Wo Waldteufel, Wehrwolf, Schakal	Where wood demons, werewolves, jackals
Ihr verruchtes Wesen treiben—	Prowl and howl among the ruins.

Schlangen, Nachtgevögel nisten	"Snakes, screech owls, and scorpions
Im verwitterten Gemäuer;	Nest in the decaying stonework;
Aus des Fensters luft'gem Bogen	From the windows' airy arches,
Schaut der Fuchs mit Wohlbehagen.	Foxes gaze and feel no danger.
Hier und da taucht auf zuweilen	"Sometimes here and there a tattered
Ein zerlumpter Knecht der Wüste,	Desert-dweller will appear
Der sein höckriges Kamehl	And will let his humpbacked camel
In dem hohen Grase weidet.	Feed upon the wild grasses.
Auf der edlen Höhe Zions,	"On the noble heights of Zion,
Wo die goldne Veste ragte,	Where the golden fortress towered,
Deren Herrlichkeiten zeugten	Bearing witness in its splendor
Von der Pracht des großen Königs:	To a great king's majesty,
Dort, von Unkraut überwuchert,	"Weeds grow lush and tall, and over-
Liegen nur noch graue Trümmer,	whelm the ruins still remaining,
Die uns ansehn schmerzhaft traurig,	Which look out at you so sadly,
Daß man glauben muß, sie weinten.	You imagine that they're weeping.
Und es heißt, sie weinten wirklich	"And the story goes that truly
Einmal in dem Jahr, an jenem	Once a year they *do* weep, on the
Neunten Tag des Monats Ab—	Ninth day of the month of Av—
Und mit thränend eignen Augen	I myself, my own eyes weeping,
Schaute ich die dicken Tropfen	"Have beheld the heavy teardrops
Aus den großen Steinen sickern,	Falling from the massive stones, and
Und ich hörte weheklagen	I have heard the broken pillars
Die gebrochnen Tempelsäulen.«—	Crying out in lamentation."
Solche fromme Pilgersagen	Such reports from saintly pilgrims
Weckten in der jungen Brust	Wakened in his ardent breast
Des Jehuda ben Halevy	A profound and constant longing
Sehnsucht nach Jerusalem.	For his love, Jerusalem.

310

320

330

FOXES GAZE AND FEEL NO DANGER

Dichtersehnsucht! ahnend, träumend	It was dream-possessed, prophetic,
Und fatal war sie, wie jene,	Ominous, as was the longing
Die auf seinem Schloß zu Blaye	Which at the château de Blaye
Einst empfand der alte Vidam,	Once possessed the noble prince and
Messer Geoffroi Rudello,	Troubadour Jaufré Rudel,
Als die Ritter, die zurück	Who, to knights returning home
Aus dem Morgenlande kehrten,	From the Holy Land, amid the
Laut beim Becherklang betheuert:	Clang of goblets, loudly swore
Ausbund aller Huld und Züchten,	That the paragon of virtue,
Perl' und Blume aller Frauen,	Pearl and flower of all women,
Sey die schöne Melisande,	Was the lovely Melisanda,
Markgräfin von Tripolis.	Margravine of Tripoli.
Jeder weiß, für diese Dame	Everybody knows how Jaufré
Schwärmte jetzt der Troubadour;	Rhapsodized about this lady,
Er besang sie, und es wurde	Sang her praise, felt life too narrow
Ihm zu eng im Schlosse Blaye.	There in his ancestral palace.
Und es trieb ihn fort. Zu Cette	So his longing drove him forth to
Schiffte er sich ein, erkrankte	Seek her. He embarked at Cette
Aber auf dem Meer, und sterbend	But grew sick on board and, close to
Kam er an zu Tripolis.	Dying, came to Tripoli.
Hier erblickt' er Melisanden	Here he gazed with love, ecstatic,
Endlich auch mit Leibesaugen,	On the lady Melisanda,
Die jedoch des Todes Schatten	But at that same moment, death
In derselben Stunde deckten.	Poured its shade upon his eyelids.
Seinen letzten Liebessang	Singing then his final love song,
Singend, starb er zu den Füßen	He expired at the feet of
Seiner Dame Melisande,	His dear lady, Melisanda,
Markgräfin von Tripolis.	Margravine of Tripoli.
Wunderbare Aehnlichkeit	Strange the similarity
In dem Schicksal beider Dichter!	In the fates of these two poets!

340

350

360

Nur daß jener erst im Alter	Only, one was old already
Seine große Wallfahrt antrat.	When he left on pilgrimage.
Auch Jehuda ben Halevy	Thus Yehuda ben Halévi
Starb zu Füßen seiner Liebsten,	At the feet of his belovèd
Und sein sterbend Haupt, es ruhte	Died and laid his head upon the
Auf den Knien Jerusalems.	Lap of his Jerusalem.

III

Nach der Schlacht bey Arabella	When the Battle of Arbéla	
Hat der große Alexander	Ended, the great Alexander	370
Land und Leute des Darius,	Stuffed the wealth of King Daríus—	
Hof und Harem, Pferde, Weiber,	Court and harem, women, horses,	
Elephanten und Dariken,	Elephants and coins and gardens,	
Kron' und Zepter, goldnen Plunder,	Crown and scepter, golden rubbish—	
Eingesteckt in seine weiten	Stuffed them leisurely inside his	
Macedon'schen Pluderhosen.	Baggy Macedonian trousers.	
In dem Zelt des großen Königs,	In the tent of the great monarch,	
Der entflohn um nicht höchstselbst	Who had fled, lest he himself be	
Gleichfalls eingesteckt zu werden,	Stuffed away like all the rest,	
Fand der junge Held ein Kästchen,	The young hero found a casket,	380
Eine kleine güldne Truhe,	An exquísite golden coffer	
Mit Miniaturbildwerken	Richly decorated with	
Und mit inkrustirten Steinen	Miniature portraits, precious	
Und Kameen reich geschmückt—	Stones, and ivory cameos.	
Dieses Kästchen, selbst ein Kleinod	This small chest, itself a treasure,	
Unschätzbaren Werthes, diente	Of inestimable value	
Zur Bewahrung von Kleinodien,	Was the case in which the king had	
Des Monarchen Leibjuwelen.	Stored his priceless body jewels.	
Letztre schenkte Alexander	Alexander gave these jewels	
An die Tapfern seines Heeres,	To the bravest of his soldiers,	390

Darob lächelnd, daß sich Männer
Kindisch freun an bunten Steinchen.

Eine kostbar schönste Gemme
Schickte er der lieben Mutter;
War der Siegelring des Cyrus,
Wurde jetzt zu einer Brosche.

Seinem alten Weltarschpauker
Aristoteles, dem sandt' er
Einen Onix für sein großes
Naturalienkabinet.

In dem Kästchen waren Perlen,
Eine wunderbare Schnur,
Die der Königin Atossa
Einst geschenkt der falsche Smerdis—

Doch die Perlen waren echt—
Und der heitre Sieger gab sie
Einer schönen Tänzerin
Aus Corinth, mit Namen Thais.

Diese trug sie in den Haaren,
Die bacchantisch aufgelöst,
In der Brandnacht, als sie tanzte
Zu Persepolis und frech

In die Königsburg geschleudert
Ihre Fackel, daß laut prasselnd
Bald die Flammenlohe aufschlug,
Wie ein Feuerwerk zum Feste.

Nach dem Tod der schönen Thais,
Die an einer babylon'schen
Krankheit starb zu Babylon,
Wurden ihre Perlen dort

Smiling that grown men, like children,
Valued little colored pebbles.

One of the most precious jewels
He bestowed upon his mother:
The great signet ring of Cyrus,
Which she made into a brooch.

And to Aristotle, his old
Bottom-thwacker, he dispatched a
Splendid onyx for his famous
Natural history collection.   400

In the casket there was also
An amazing string of pearls, which
Once had been the gift of Smerdis
(The false one) to Queen Atossa.

But the pearls themselves were real,
And the cheerful victor gave them
To a very pretty Greek
Dancer by the name of Thaïs.

This girl wore them in her lovely
Hair that streamed like a bacchante's   410
In Persépolis that night when,
As she danced, she impudently

Flung her torch into the palace;
With a crackle, it blazed up and
Quickly started to explode like
Fireworks on New Year's Eve.

On the death of lovely Thaïs,
Who had caught the Babylonian
Clap and had expired there, the
Celebrated pearls were promptly   420

Auf dem Börsensaal vergantert.
Sie erstand ein Pfaff aus Memphis,
Der sie nach Egypten brachte,
Wo sie später auf dem Putztisch

Der Cleopatra erschienen,
Die die schönste Perl' zerstampft
Und mit Wein vermischt verschluckte,
Um Antonius zu foppen.

Mit dem letzten Omayaden
Kam die Perlenschnur nach Spanien,
Und sie schlängelte am Turban
Des Califen zu Corduva.

Abderam der Dritte trug sie
Als Brustschleife beim Turnier,
Wo er dreyzig goldne Ringe
Und das Herz Zuleimas stach.

Nach dem Fall der Mohrenherrschaft
Gingen zu den Christen über
Auch die Perlen, und geriethen
In den Kronschatz von Castilien.

Die kathol'schen Majestäten
Span'scher Königinnen schmückten
Sich damit bey Hoffestspielen,
Stiergefechten, Prozessionen,

So wie auch Autodafés,
Wo sie, auf Balkonen sitzend,
Sich erquickten am Geruche
Von gebratnen alten Juden.

Sold off at a public auction.
A discerning priest from Memphis
Bought them, took them back to Egypt,
Where they later made their way to

Cleopatra's dressing table;
She plucked out the rarest pearl, dis-
solved it in some wine and drank it,
Just to tease Mark Antony.

After the Omáyyads conquered
Spain, the necklace found itself in   430
Cordoba and coiled around the
Caliph's turban, like a snake.

Ábderam the Third then wore it
As a breast knot at the tourney,
Where he pierced through thirty golden
Rings and through Zuleima's heart.

When the Moorish kingdom crumbled,
The pearl necklace also passed on
Into Christian hands and wound up
In the crown jewels of Castile.   440

Their Most Catholic Majesties, the
Queens of Spain, would always wear them
At the court's festivities, at
Bullfights, and at Church processions,

And at the autos-da-fé, where,
Sitting on their balconies, they
Fanned themselves and took refreshment
In the smell of old Jews roasting.

THE QUEENS OF SPAIN WOULD ALWAYS WEAR [THE PEARLS] . . . AT THE AUTOS-DA-FÉ

Späterhin gab Mendizabel,
Satans-Enkel, diese Perlen
In Versatz, um der Finanzen
Defizit damit zu decken.

An dem Hof der Tuilerien
Kam die Schnur zuletzt zum Vorschein,
Und sie schimmerte am Halse
Der Baronin Salomon.

So erging's den schönen Perlen.
Minder abentheuerlich
Ging's dem Kästchen, dies behielt
Alexander für sich selber.

Er verschloß darin die Lieder
Des ambrosischen Homeros,
Seines Lieblings, und zu Häupten
Seines Bettes in der Nacht

Stand das Kästchen—schlief der König,
Stiegen draus hervor der Helden
Lichte Bilder, und sie schlichen
Gaukelnd sich in seine Träume.

Andre Zeiten, andre Vögel—
Ich, ich liebte weiland gleichfalls
Die Gesänge von den Thaten
Des Peliden, des Odysseus.

Damals war so sonnengoldig
Und so purpurn mir zu Muthe,
Meine Stirn' umkränzte Weinlaub,
Und es tönten die Fanfaren—

Later, Señor Mendizábal
Satan's grandson, pawned the pearls to   450
Cancel certain deficits that
Weighed upon the Queen's finances.

Last, the pearl strand was presented
At the royal court in Paris,
Shimmering on the neck of the dis-
tinguished Baroness von Rothschild.

So much for the lovely pearls.
Less adventurous were the fortunes
Of the casket. Alexander
Kept it for his private uses,   460

And inside he put the epics
Sung by the immortal Homer,
His belovèd, and at night, just
By his pillow, at his bedside,

Stood the chest; as he lay sleeping,
Radiant forms of heroes rose up
From the parchment scrolls and glided
Into Alexander's dreams.

Other times have other birdsongs—
I, too, loved them, long ago, those   470
Songs about the noble actions
Of Achilles, of Odysseus.

Then my spirits were as golden
As the sun, my heart exulted,
And my brow was wreathed with vine leaves,
And the fanfares kept resounding.

Still davon—gebrochen liegt
Jetzt mein stolzer Siegeswagen,
Und die Panther, die ihn zogen,
Sind verreckt, so wie die Weiber,

Die mit Pauk' und Zimbelklängen
Mich umtanzten, und ich selbst
Wälze mich am Boden elend,
Krüppelelend—still davon—

Still davon—es ist die Rede
Von dem Kästchen des Darius,
Und ich dacht in meinem Sinne:
Käm ich in Besitz des Kästchens,

Und mich zwänge nicht Finanznoth,
Gleich dasselbe zu versilbern,
So verschlösse ich darin
Die Gedichte unsres Rabbi—

Des Jehuda ben Halevy
Festgesänge, Klagelieder,
Die Ghaselen, Reisebilder
Seiner Wallfahrt—alles ließ' ich

Von dem besten Zophar schreiben
Auf der reinsten Pergamenthaut,
Und ich legte diese Handschrift
In das kleine goldne Kästchen.

Dieses stellt' ich auf den Tisch
Neben meinem Bett, und kämen
Dann die Freunde und erstaunten
Ob der Pracht der kleinen Truhe,

Hush now! Fallen, smashed to pieces,
Lies my proud triumphal chariot,
And the panthers that once drew it
All are dead, the women also   480

Who with drums and clash of cymbals
Danced around me. I myself am
Writhing on the floor here, wretched,
Crippled, and in anguish—hush now—

That's enough. We just were speaking
Of the casket of Daríus,
And the thought occurred to me that
If I ever gained possession

Of that casket, and I weren't
Forced to turn it into cash,   490
I would keep enclosed within it
All the poems of our rabbi—

All Yehuda ben Halévi's
Songs for feast days, lamentations,
Hymns, ghazals, the poems of his
Pilgrimage—and I would order

A great scribe to write them out, in
Black ink on the purest parchment,
And would lay the manuscript in-
side the little golden casket.   500

I would put it on a table
By my bed, and when my friends came
And they looked, astonished, at the
Splendors of the little casket—

I WOULD ORDER A GREAT SCRIBE TO WRITE THEM OUT

Ob den seltnen Basrelièffen,
Die so winzig, doch vollendet
Sind zugleich und ob den großen
Inkrustirten Edelsteinen—

Lächelnd würd' ich ihnen sagen:
Das ist nur die rohe Schale,
Die den bessern Schatz verschließet—
Hier in diesem Kästchen liegen

Diamanten, deren Lichter
Abglanz, Wiederschein des Himmels,
Herzblutglühende Rubinen,
Fleckenlose Turkoasen,

Auch Smaragde der Verheißung,
Perlen, reiner noch als jene,
Die der Königin Atossa
Einst geschenkt der falschen Smerdis,

Und die späterhin geschmücket
Alle Notabilitäten
Dieser mondumkreisten Erde,
Thais und Cleopatra,

Isispriester, Mohrenfürsten,
Auch Hispaniens Königinnen.
Und zuletzt die hochverehrte
Frau Baronin Salomon—

Diese weltberühmten Perlen,
Sie sind nur der bleiche Schleim
Eines armen Austerthiers,
Das im Meergrund blöde kränkelt:

At the precious bas-reliefs,
So minúte and yet so perfect,
And at all the large and lustrous
Jewels that adorn the cover—

With a smile I would tell them,
What you see is a crude shell   510
That contains a finer treasure.
Here within this casket lie

Diamonds whose rare effulgence
Mirrors back the light of heaven,
Rubies glowing red as heart's blood,
Turquoises of flawless beauty,

Emeralds that shine with promise,
Pearls far purer than the pearls that
Once had been the gift of Smerdis
(The false one) to Queen Atossa   520

And that later ornamented
Many great celebrities
On this moon-encircled planet:
Thaïs first, then Cleopatra,

Priests of Isis, Moorish princes,
And the queens of old Hispania,
And at last the neck of the dis-
tinguished Baroness von Rothschild.

These world-famous pearls are just the
Hardened slime from some poor oyster   530
Suffering from some stupid illness
At the bottom of the ocean;

Doch die Perlen hier im Kästchen	But the pearls inside this casket
Sind entquollen einer schönen	Come forth from a rare and lovely
Menschenseele, die noch tiefer,	Human soul, a soul far deeper
Abgrundtiefer als das Weltmeer—	Than the vast abyss of ocean—
Denn es sind die Thränenperlen	For they are the bitter teardrops
Des Jehuda ben Halevy,	Of Yehuda ben Halévi,
Die er ob dem Untergang	Which he wept for the destruction
Von Jerusalem geweinet—	Of his love, Jerusalem,
Perlenthränen, die verbunden	Pearl-like tears that, strung together
Durch des Reimes goldnen Faden,	On the golden thread of rhyme,
Aus der Dichtkunst güldnen Schmiede	Turned into a treasure when they
Als ein Lied hervorgegangen.	Later issued as a poem.
Dieses Perlenthränenlied	This great song, the poet's teardrops,
Ist die vielberühmte Klage,	Is the famous lamentation
Die gesungen wird in allen	Sung in all the tents of Jacob,
Weltzerstreuten Zelten Jakobs	Scattered throughout all the world,
An dem neunten Tag des Monats,	On the ninth day of the month of
Der geheißen Ab, dem Jahrstag	Av, the anniversary date
Von Jerusalems Zerstörung	Of Jerusalem's destruction
Durch den Titus Vespasianus.	By the Roman general Titus.
Ja, das ist das Zionslied,	Yes, this is the song of Zion
Das Jehuda ben Halevy	That Yehuda ben Halévi
Sterbend auf den heil'gen Trümmern	Sang about Jerusalem,
Von Jerusalem gesungen—	As he died among the ruins,
Barfuß und im Büßerkittel	Barefoot, dressed in penitential
Saß er dorten auf dem Bruchstück	Garments, sitting on the fragment
Einer umgestürzten Säule;—	Of a fallen marble pillar.
Bis zur Brust herunter fiel	Gray hair fell below his shoulders

540

550

560

OF JERUSALEM'S DESTRUCTION BY THE ROMAN GENERAL TITUS

A SAVAGE ARAB HORSEMAN . . . LIKE A WINGÈD PHANTOM

Wie ein greiser Wald sein Haupthaar,
Abentheuerlich beschattend
Das bekümmert bleiche Antlitz
Mit den geisterhaften Augen—

Also saß er und er sang,
Wie ein Seher aus der Vorzeit
Anzuschaun—dem Grab entstiegen
Schien Jeremias, der Alte—

Das Gevögel der Ruinen
Zähmte schier der wilde Schmerzlaut
Des Gesanges, und die Geyer
Nahten horchend, fast mitleidig—

Doch ein frecher Sarazene
Kam desselben Wegs geritten,
Hoch zu Roß, im Bug sich wiegend
Und die blanke Lanze schwingend—

In die Brust des armen Sängers
Stieß er diesen Todesspeer,
Und er jagte rasch von dannen,
Wie ein Schattenbild beflügelt.

Ruhig floß das Blut des Rabbi,
Ruhig seinen Sang zu Ende
Sang er, und sein sterbeletzter
Seufzer war Jerusalem!—

Eine alte Sage meldet,
Jener Sarazene sey
Gar kein böser Mensch gewesen,
Sondern ein verkappter Engel,

Like a withered, overhanging
Forest, casting ghostly shadows
On those pale and anguished features
With the otherworldly eyes.

There he sat among the ruins,
Singing, and he seemed an ancient
Prophet, as if Jeremiah
Had arisen from his grave.

And his song of wild bereavement
Tamed the birds amid the ruins,   570
And the vultures came and listened,
As if prompted by compassion.

But a savage Arab horseman
Galloped down that very pathway,
Rocked back on his lofty steed, and
Thrust his lance into the bosom

Of the poet as he sat there
Singing his heartbroken verses,
And then quickly galloped off and
Vanished, like a wingèd phantom.   580

Calmly flowed the rabbi's blood, and
Calmly did he sing his lyric,
Till he died there, and his very
Last word was *Jerusalem*.

But an ancient legend has it
That the evil Saracen was
Not, in fact, a human being
But an angel in disguise,

Der vom Himmel ward gesendet,
Gottes Liebling zu entrücken
Dieser Erde, und zu fördern
Ohne Qual in's Reich der Sel'gen.

Droben, heißt es, harrte seiner
Ein Empfang der schmeichelhaft
Ganz besonders für den Dichter,
Eine himmlische Sürprise.

Festlich kam das Chor der Engel
Ihm entgegen mit Musik,
Und als Hymne grüßten ihn
Seine eignen Verse, jenes

Synagogen-Hochzeitcarmen,
Jene Sabbath-Hymenäen,
Mit den jauchzend wohlbekannten
Melodieen—welche Töne!

Englein bliesen auf Hauboen,
Englein spielten Violine,
Andre strichen auch die Bratsche
Oder schlugen Pauk' und Zimbel.

Und das sang und klang so lieblich,
Und so lieblich in den weiten
Himmelsräumen wiederhallt es:
Lecho Daudi Likras Kalle.

IV

Meine Frau ist nicht zufrieden
Mit dem vorigen Capitel,
Ganz besonders in Bezug
Auf das Kästchen des Darius.

Who was sent direct from heaven
To deliver God's belovèd
From this earth and lift him, painless,
To the kingdom of the blessed.

Up there, we are told, was waiting
A reception for the poet,
Flattering to his amour propre,
A celestial surprise.

Cheerfully a choir of angels
Came to meet him, playing music,
And the hymn they sang to greet him
Was his own: the very verses

He had written for the Sabbath,
Sung in all the synagogues, a
Wedding song, with the familiar
Joyful tune—but ah, what music!

Little angels played on oboes,
Others violins, still others
Drew their bows across the strings of
Cellos, or beat drums or cymbals.

And the song rang out so sweetly
And so sweetly resonated
Through the vast expanse of heaven:
Lécho, dódi, líkras kálle!

IV

My dear wife is not too happy
With the chapter I just finished,
Most especially with reference
To the casket of Daríus.

LITTLE ANGELS PLAYED ON OBOES, OTHERS VIOLINS

Fast mit Bitterkeit bemerkt sie:	Almost bitterly she tells me
Daß ein Ehemann, der wahrhaft	That a husband who was truly
Religiöse sey, das Kästchen	Thoughtful would immediately
Gleich zu Gelde machen würde,	Turn the casket into money 620
Um damit für seine arme	So that he could purchase for his
Legitime Ehegattin	Poor and lawful wedded wife
Einen Kaschemir zu kaufen,	The attractive cashmere shawl
Dessen sie so sehr bedürfe.	That she was so much in need of.
Der Jehuda ben Halevy,	And Yehuda ben Halévi,
Meinte sie, der sey hinlänglich	So she told me, would be honored
Ehrenvoll bewahrt in einem	Quite enough by being kept in
Schönen Futteral von Pappe	An attractive cardboard box
Mit chinesisch eleganten	With some elegant Chinese-y
Arabesken, wie die hübschen	Arabesques, just like those pretty 630
Bonbonnièren von Marquis	Bonbon boxes from "Marquis" in
Im Passage Panorama.	Le passage des Panoramas.
Sonderbar!—setzt sie hinzu—	It is awfully strange, she added,
Daß ich niemals nennen hörte	That I never heard of him, if
Diesen großen Dichternamen,	He was such a famous poet,
Den Jehuda ben Halevy.	Your Yehuda ben Halévi.
Liebstes Kind, gab ich zur Antwort,	Dearest child, I answered, this quite
Solche holde Ignoranz,	Charming ignorance of yours
Sie bekundet die Lakunen	Only shows the dreadful weakness
Der französischen Erziehung,	Of the education offered 640
Der Pariser Pensionate,	In the boarding schools of Paris,
Wo die Mädchen, diese künft'gen	Where the girls, those future mothers
Mütter eines freyen Volkes,	Of a freedom-loving people,
Ihren Unterricht genießen—	Are supposed to be instructed.

THOSE PRETTY BONBON BOXES FROM "MARQUIS"

Alte Mumien, ausgestopfte	Ancient mummies, stuffed Egyptian
Pharaonen von Egypten,	Pharaohs, Clovis and the other
Merovinger Schattenkön'ge,	Merovingian shadow kings,
Ungepuderte Perücken,	Periwigs sans powder, and the
Auch die Zopfmonarchen Chinas,	Pigtailed emperors of China
Porzellanpagodenkaiser—	With their porcelain pagodas—
Alle lernen sie auswendig,	All of this they learn by heart, these
Kluge Mädchen, aber Himmel—	Clever girls. But oh, ye heavens,
Fragt man sie nach großen Namen	If they're asked about the poets
Aus dem großen Goldzeitalter	From the glorious golden age of
Der arabisch-althispanisch	Ancient Arab-Spanish-Jewish
Jüdischen Poetenschule,	Poetry, that school of genius,
Fragt man nach dem Dreygestirn,	If they're asked about the three great
Nach Jehuda ben Halevy,	Stars—Yehuda ben Halévi,
Nach dem Salomon Gabirol	Solomon Gabírol, or the
Und dem Moses Iben Esra—	Third one, Moses ibn Ezra—
Fragt man nach dergleichen Namen,	If they're asked about these poets,
Dann mit großen Augen schaun	Then the little maidens stare, with
Uns die Kleinen an—alsdann	Great big eyes—a herd of heifers
Stehn am Berge die Ochsinnen.	Startled, looking up with cow eyes.
Rathen möcht' ich dir, Geliebte,	I advise you now, belovèd,
Nachzuholen das Versäumte	To make up for this omission
Und hebräisch zu erlernen—	And to learn the Hebrew language.
Laß Theater und Conzerte,	Leave your theater and your concerts;
Widme ein'ge Jahre solchem	After several years of study,
Studium, du kannst alsdann	You'll be far enough along to
Im Originale lesen	Read, in the original,
Iben Esra und Gabirol	Ibn Ezra and Gabírol,

650

660

670

Und versteht sich den Halevy,
Das Triumvirat der Dichtkunst,
Das dem Saitenspiel Davidis
Einst entlockt die schönsten Laute.

Alcharisi—der, ich wette,
Dir nicht minder unbekannt ist,
Ob er gleich, französ'scher Witzbold,
Den Hariri überwitzelt

Im Gebiete der Makame,
Und ein Voltairianer war
Schon sechs hundert Jahr vor Voltair'—
Jener Alcharisi sagte:

»Durch Gedanken glänzt Gabirol
Und gefällt zumeist dem Denker,
Iben Esra glänzt durch Kunst
Und behagt weit mehr dem Künstler—

Aber beider Eigenschaften
Hat Jehuda ben Halevy,
Und er ist ein großer Dichter
Und ein Liebling aller Menschen.«

Iben Esra war ein Freund
Und ich glaube auch ein Vetter
Des Jehuda ben Halevy,
Der in seinem Wanderbuche

Schmerzlich klagt, wie er vergebens
In Granada aufgesucht hat
Seinen Freund, und nur den Bruder
Dorten fand, den Medikus,

And, of course, the great Halévi—
The triumvirate of versecraft—
Who upon the harp of David
Played the most exquísite music.

Al-Harízi—who, I bet, is
Just as unfamiliar to you,
Though he was as witty as a
Frenchman, and he overwitted   680

Al-Haríri in his word games
And was a Voltairean, six
Hundred years before Voltaire was—
Well, this al-Harízi said,

"In the realm of thought, Gabírol
Shines and gratifies the thinker;
Ibn Ezra shines through art, and
Is most pleasing to the artist;

"But Yehuda ben Halévi
Has embodied both these virtues,   690
And he is a mighty poet
Rightfully beloved by all."

Ibn Ezra was a friend, and
Was as well, I think, a cousin
Of Yehuda ben Halévi—
Who laments that in Granada,

When he went there on a journey
Looking for his friend, he couldn't
Find him anywhere, but only
Found his brother, the physician   700

Rabbi Meyer, auch ein Dichter	Rabbi Meyer, who was also
Und der Vater jener Schönen,	Father of that pretty girl who
Die mit hoffnungsloser Flamme	Lit the flames of hopeless passion
Iben Esras Herz entzunden—	In the heart of ibn Ezra.
Um das Mühmchen zu vergessen,	To forget his little niece, he
Griff er nach dem Wanderstabe,	Took his pilgrim's staff and wandered
Wie so mancher der Collegen;	Like so many of his comrades,
Lebte unstät, heimatlos.	Lived for years unsettled, homeless.
Pilgernd nach Jerusalem,	Traveling to Jerusalem,
Ueberfielen ihn Tartaren,	He was set upon by Tartars,
Die an einen Gaul gebunden	Who then strapped him to a nag and
Ihn nach ihren Steppen schleppten.	Dragged him to their native steppes.
Mußte Dienste dort verrichten,	There he had to render service
Die nicht würdig eines Rabbi	Quite unworthy of a rabbi,
Und noch wen'ger eines Dichters,	Still unworthier of a poet—
Mußte nämlich Kühe melken.	There, in short, he milked the cattle.
Einstens, als er unterm Bauche	Once, at work, as he was leaning
Einer Kuh gekauert saß,	Forward under a cow's belly,
Ihre Euter hastig fingernd,	Briskly pulling at the udders,
Daß die Milch floß in den Zuber—	Splashing milk into the bucket,
Eine Posizion, unwürdig	An undignified position
Eines Rabbis, eines Dichters—	For a rabbi or a poet,
Da befiel ihn tiefe Wehmuth,	He was overwhelmed with such great
Und er fing zu singen an,	Sorrow that he had to sing, and
Und er sang so schön und lieblich,	He sang out so beautifully
Daß der Chan, der Fürst der Horde,	That the Khan, the horde's commander,
Der vorbey ging, ward gerühret	Passing by, was moved and granted
Und die Freyheit gab dem Sklaven.	Freedom to the wretched slave.

710

720

Auch Geschenke gab er ihm,
Einen Fuchspelz, eine lange
Sarazenenmandoline
Und das Zehrgeld für die Heimkehr.

Dichterschicksal! böser Unstern,
Der die Söhne des Apollo
Tödtlich nergelt, und sogar
Ihren Vater nicht verschont hat,

Als er hinter Daphnen laufend
Statt des weißen Nymphenleibes
Nur den Lorbeerbaum erfaßte,
Er, der göttliche Schlemihl!

Ja, der hohe Delphier ist
Ein Schlemihl, und gar der Lorbeer,
Der so stolz die Stirne krönet,
Ist ein Zeichen des Schlemihlthums.

Was das Wort Schlemihl bedeutet,
Wissen wir. Hat doch Chamisso
Ihm das Bürgerrecht in Deutschland
Längst verschafft, dem Worte nemlich.

Aber unbekannt geblieben,
Wie des heil'gen Niles Quellen,
Ist sein Ursprung; hab' darüber
Nachgegrübelt manche Nacht.

Zu Berlin vor vielen Jahren
Wandt' ich mich deßhalb an unsern
Freund Chamisso, suchte Auskunft
Beim Dekane der Schlemihle.

And he gave him gifts as well: an
Unused fox skin, an ornate   730
Five-stringed Arab mandolin, and
All his traveling expenses.

Fate of poets! Evil star that
Persecutes Apollo's sons
With your grudging, lethal rays and
Didn't even spare their father,

When he, in pursuit of Daphne,
Reaching for the nymph's white body
Threw his arms around some tree bark—
Though a god, a true shlemiel!   740

Yes, the lofty Delphic god is
A shlemiel; the very laurel
That so proudly crowns his forehead
Is a sign of his shlemieldom.

Everybody knows the word *shle-*
miel. Chamisso long ago
Introduced it and secured its
Civil rights in Germany.

But its origin is still as
Little known as are the sources   750
Of the Nile—I have puzzled
Over this for many a night.

Years ago, in fact, I traveled
To Berlin to see Chamisso
And to ask for information
From the dean of all shlemiels,

Doch er konnt' mich nicht befried'gen
Und verwies mich drob an Hitzig,
Der ihm den Familiennamen
Seines schattenlosen Peters

Einst verrathen. Alsbald nahm ich
Eine Droschke und ich rollte
Zu dem Criminalrath Hitzig,
Welcher eh'mals Itzig hieß—

Als er noch ein Itzig war,
Träumte ihm, er säh' geschrieben
An dem Himmel seinen Namen
Und davor den Buchstab H.

»Was bedeutet dieses H?«
Frug er sich—»etwa Herr Itzig
Oder Heil'ger Itzig? Heil'ger
Ist ein schöner Titel—aber

In Berlin nicht passend«—Endlich
Grübelnsmüd' nannt' er sich Hitzig,
Und nur die Getreuen wußten:
In dem Hitzig steckt ein Heil'ger.

Heil'ger Hitzig! sprach ich also,
Als ich zu ihm kam, Sie sollen
Mir die Etymologie
Von dem Wort Schlemihl erklären.

Viel Umschweife nahm der Heil'ge,
Konnte sich nicht recht erinnern,
Eine Ausflucht nach der andern,
Immer christlich—Bis mir endlich,

But he couldn't satisfy me,
So he passed me on to Hitzig,
Who had been the first to tell him
What this man who sold his shadow's   760

Surname was. I took a droshky
Right away and rolled off to the
Court Investigator Hitzig,
Who was Itzig in the old days.

Back when he was still an Itzig,
In a dream he saw his surname
Blazoned in the heavens, and be-
fore it stood the letter H.

And he asked, "What is the meaning
Of this H? Perhaps *Herr* Itzig?   770
Holy Itzig? 'Holy' is a
Splendid title, but not suited

"For Berlin." At last, exhausted
By this puzzle, he took on the
Name of Hitzig. (Just the faithful
Realize his saintly nature.)

"Holy Hitzig," I addressed him
When I saw him, "would you tell me
What the etymology
Of this Yiddish word *shlemiel* is?"   780

Then the saint began to hem and
Haw, he said he couldn't quite re-
member, and piled up excuses
In his oh-so-Christian way,

HITZIG, WHO WAS ITZIG IN THE OLD DAYS

Endlich alle Knöpfe rissen
An der Hose der Geduld,
Und ich anfing so zu fluchen,
So gottlästerlich zu fluchen,

Daß der fromme Pietist,
Leichenblaß und beineschlotternd,
Unverzüglich mir willfahrte
Und mir Folgendes erzählte:

»In der Bibel ist zu lesen,
Als zur Zeit der Wüstenwandrung
Israel sich oft erlustigt
Mit den Töchtern Kanaans,

Da geschah es, daß der Pinhas
Sahe wie der edle Simri
Buhlschaft trieb mit einem Weibsbild
Aus dem Stamm der Kananiter,

Und alsbald ergriff er zornig
Seinen Speer und hat den Simri
Auf der Stelle todtgestochen—
Also heißt es in der Bibel.

Aber mündlich überliefert
Hat im Volke sich die Sage,
Daß es nicht der Simri war,
Den des Pinhas Speer getroffen,

Sondern daß der Blinderzürnte,
Statt des Sünders, unversehens
Einen ganz Unschuld'gen traf,
Den Schlemihl ben Zuri Schadday.«—

Dieser nun, Schlemihl I,
Ist der Ahnherr des Geschlechtes

Till at last I popped the buttons
On the trousers of my patience,
And I started swearing loudly,
With such blasphemous abandon

That the pious fellow grew
Deathly pale, his knees shook, and he   790
Promptly granted what I'd asked for
And delivered this account:

"In the Bible it is written
That the Israelites who wandered
In the desert often dallied
With the lusty girls of Canaan.

"So it came to pass that one day
Pinkhas saw the noble Zimri
Having sex (to put it bluntly)
With a Canaanitish female.   800

"Livid, he picked up his spear and
Walking up to Zimri, stuck it
Through his back and out his belly—
So the Holy Bible tells us.

"But there is a legend, handed
Down for untold generations,
Saying that it wasn't Zimri
Whom the spear of Pinkhas killed:

"Rather, blind with rage and striking
Randomly, he missed the mark and   810
Killed a total innocent
Named Shlemiel ben Zurisháddai."

So this man, Shlemiel the First,
Is the patron ancestor of

Derer von Schlemihl. Wir stammen
Von Schlemihl ben Zuri Schadday.

Freylich keine Heldenthaten
Meldet man von ihm, wir kennen
Nur den Namen und wir wissen
Daß er ein Schlemihl gewesen.

Doch geschätzet wird ein Stammbaum
Nicht ob seinen guten Früchten,
Sondern nur ob seinem Alter—
Drey Jahrtausend zählt der unsre!

Jahre kommen und vergehen—
Drey Jahrtausende verflossen,
Seit gestorben unser Ahnherr,
Herr Schlemihl ben Zuri Schadday.

Längst ist auch der Pinhas todt—
Doch sein Speer hat sich erhalten,
Und wir hören ihn beständig
Ueber unsre Häupter schwirren.

Und die besten Herzen trifft er—
Wie Jehuda ben Halevy,
Traf er Moses Iben Esra,
Und er traf auch den Gabirol—

Den Gabirol, diesen treuen
Gottgeweihten Minnesänger,
Diese fromme Nachtigall
Deren Rose Gott gewesen—

Diese Nachtigall, die zärtlich
Ihre Liebeslieder sang
In der Dunkelheit der gotisch
Mittelalterlichen Nacht!

All shlemiels. We're all descended
From Shlemiel ben Zurisháddai.

No heroic deed has ever
Been reported of him; all we
Know about him is his name and
That he was a true shlemiel.   820

Still, one's family tree is valued
Not because of its good fruit but
Its antiquity, and ours
Goes back for three thousand years.

Years keep coming and dissolving.
Three millennia have passed
Since the death of our first father,
Herr Shlemiel ben Zurisháddai.

Pinkhas has been dead a long time
Also, but his spear is with us   830
Still, and we can hear it whirring
Not too far above our heads.

And it stabs the noblest hearts,
Like Yehuda ben Halévi's,
And like Moses ibn Ezra's,
And Gabírol's heart as well,

This sincere and God-devoted
Troubadour, this passionately
Reverent Jewish nightingale, whose
Only true love was the Lord—   840

Nightingale who tenderly
Sang out his resplendent love songs
In the densest darkness of the
Gothic medieval night.

Unerschrocken, unbekümmert	Undiscouraged and untroubled
Ob den Fratzen und Gespenstern,	By the goblins and the phantoms,
Ob dem Wust von Tod und Wahnsinn,	By the maze of death and madness
Die gespukt in jener Nacht—	Haunting people in that night,

Sie, die Nachtigall, sie dachte	This sweet nightingale thought only	
Nur an ihren göttlich Liebsten,	Of the God whom he adored, to	850
Dem sie ihre Liebe schluchzte,	Whom he sobbed his ardent love, and	
Den ihr Lobgesang verherrlicht!—	Whom his hymns of praise exalted.	

Dreyzig Lenze sah Gabirol	Only thirty years Gabírol
Hier auf Erden, aber Fama	Lived here on this earth, but Fame
Ausposaunte seines Namens	Through all lands proclaimed his timeless
Herrlichkeit durch alle Lande.	Glory with her golden trumpet.

Zu Corduba, wo er wohnte,	In the town of Cordoba there	
War ein Mohr sein nächster Nachbar,	Lived a Moor, his next-door neighbor,	
Welcher gleichfalls Verse machte	Who wrote verses, too, and envied	
Und des Dichters Ruhm beneidet'.	Our great poet's reputation.	860

Hörte er den Dichter singen,	When he heard the poet singing,
Schwoll dem Mohren gleich die Galle,	He would feel his bile rise, and
Und der Lieder Süße wurde	Every sweetness of the song was
Bittrer Wermuth für den Neidhart.	Bitter wormwood in his mouth.

Er verlockte den Verhaßten	He enticed his hated neighbor
Nächtlich in sein Haus, erschlug ihn	To his house by night and killed him,
Dorten und vergrub den Leichnam	And behind the house he buried
Hinterm Hause in dem Garten.	The dead body in the garden.

Aber siehe! aus dem Boden,	But behold now! From the ground	
Wo die Leiche eingescharrt war,	Where the body had been hidden,	870
Wuchs hervor ein Feigenbaum	Right away there grew a fig tree	
Von der wunderbarsten Schönheit.	Of an awesome loveliness.	

A FIG TREE OF AN AWESOME LOVELINESS

Seine Frucht war seltsam länglich
Und von seltsam würz'ger Süße;
Wer davon genoß, versank
In ein träumerisch Entzücken.

In dem Volke ging darüber
Viel Gerede und Gemunkel,
Das am End zu den erlauchten
Ohren des Chalifen kam.

Dieser prüfte eigenzüngig
Jenes Feigenphänomen,
Und ernannte eine strenge
Untersuchungscommission.

Man verfuhr summarisch. Sechzig
Bambushiebe auf die Sohlen
Gab man gleich dem Herrn des Baumes,
Welcher eingestand die Unthat.

Darauf riß man auch den Baum
Mit den Wurzeln aus dem Boden,
Und zum Vorschein kam die Leiche
Des erschlagenen Gabirol.

Diese ward mit Pomp bestattet
Und betrauert von den Brüdern;
An demselben Tage henkte
Man den Mohren zu Corduba.

Strangely long its fruit was, and its
Sweetness tasted strangely spicy.
Those who ate of it sank swooning
In an otherworldly rapture.

And because of this the people
Started whispering and talking,
Till before too long the rumor
Reached the Caliph's noble ears. 880

Single-tongued, the Caliph tested
This strange fig phenomenon
And appointed a commission
To investigate more closely.

Right away they asked some questions
Of the neighbor, beating him
On his soles with sixty lashes,
And the man confessed his crime.

Then they hurried to the fig tree,
Pulled it from the gaping earth, and 890
There, beneath the tree roots, lay the
Murdered body of Gabírol.

This with pomp and circumstance was
Buried, amid universal
Mourning, and the murderer was
Hanged that day in Cordoba.

—TRANSLATED BY STEPHEN MITCHELL

Disputazion

In der Aula zu Toledo
Klingen schmetternd die Fanfaren;
Zu dem geistlichen Turney
Wallt das Volk in bunten Schaaren.

Das ist nicht ein weltlich Stechen,
Keine Eisenwaffe blitzet—
Eine Lanze ist das Wort,
Das scholastisch scharf gespitzet.

Nicht galante Paladins
Fechten hier, nicht Damendiener—
Dieses Kampfes Ritter sind
Kapuziner und Rabbiner.

Statt des Helmes tragen sie
Schabbesdeckel und Kapuzen;
Scapulier und Arbekanfeß
Sind der Harnisch, drob sie trutzen.

Welches ist der wahre Gott?
Ist es der Hebräer starrer
Großer Eingott, dessen Kämpe
Rabbi Juda, der Navarrer?

Oder ist es der dreyfalt'ge
Liebegott der Christianer,
Dessen Kämpe Frater Jose,
Gardian der Franziskaner?

Disputation

In the great hall of Toledo,
Trumpets ring out in the air
To announce a holy contest
As a crowd assembles there.

This is not a clash of lances,
Or of sabers forged of steel.
The combatants' only weapons
Are the sharpened words they wield.

These opponents are not heroes
Clad in armor head to toe.   10
They are Capuchins and rabbis,
Full of what they think they know.

Some are dressed in simple cassocks
Plainly woven, brown or green.
Yarmulkes adorn the rabbis,
Swords are nowhere to be seen.

Is the Hebrews' God the greater,
Ruling sternly from afar,
Here extolled by His defender,
Rabbi Judah of Navarre?   20

Will the Christians' threefold godhead
Win the challenge on this day,
Represented by His spokesman,
The Franciscan Don José?

TRUMPETS RING

ARE THE SHARPENED WORDS THEY WIELD

THEY ARE CAPUCHINS AND RABBIS

RABBI JUDAH OF NAVARRE

FRANCISCAN DON JOSÉ

Durch die Macht der Argumente,
Durch der Logik Kettenschlüsse
Und Citate von Autoren,
Die man anerkennen müsse,

Will ein jeder Kämpe seinen
Gegner *ad absurdum* führen
Und die wahre Götlichkeit
Seines Gottes demonstriren.

Festgestellt ist: daß derjen'ge,
Der im Streit ward überwunden,
Seines Gegners Religion
Anzunehmen sey verbunden,

Daß der Jude sich der Taufe
Heil'gem Sakramente füge,
Und im Gegentheil der Christ
Der Beschneidung unterliege.

Jedem von den beiden Kämpen
Beygesellt sind elf Genossen,
Die zu theilen sein Geschick
Sind in Freud und Leid entschlossen.

Glaubenssicher sind die Mönche
Von des Gardians Geleitschaft,
Halten schon Weihwasserkübel
Für die Taufe in Bereitschaft,

Schwingen schon die Sprengelbesen
Und die blanken Räucherfässer—
Ihre Gegner unterdessen
Wetzen die Beschneidungsmesser.

Who will make the best assertions
In their spirited debate,
As they quote from ancient scholars
As of yet not out-of-date?

Which of them will lead the other
Straight into absurdity   30
As he demonstrates the power
Of his chosen deity?

It's already been determined,
And on this they've both agreed,
That the loser of this contest
Must adopt his rival's creed—

That the rabbi, without protest,
Will be presently baptized,
While the Christian, if defeated,
Will be shortly circumcised.   40

Each contender is supported
By eleven stalwart mates
Who will share their comrade's fortune
In this fiercest of debates.

So convinced are the Franciscans
That the monk will take control,
They've prepared the holy water
And have filled the votive bowl.

On the other hand, the Hebrews
Are completely unafraid   50
And show confidence by sharpening
The circumcision blade.

THAT THE RABBI, WITHOUT PROTEST, WILL BE PRESENTLY BAPTIZED

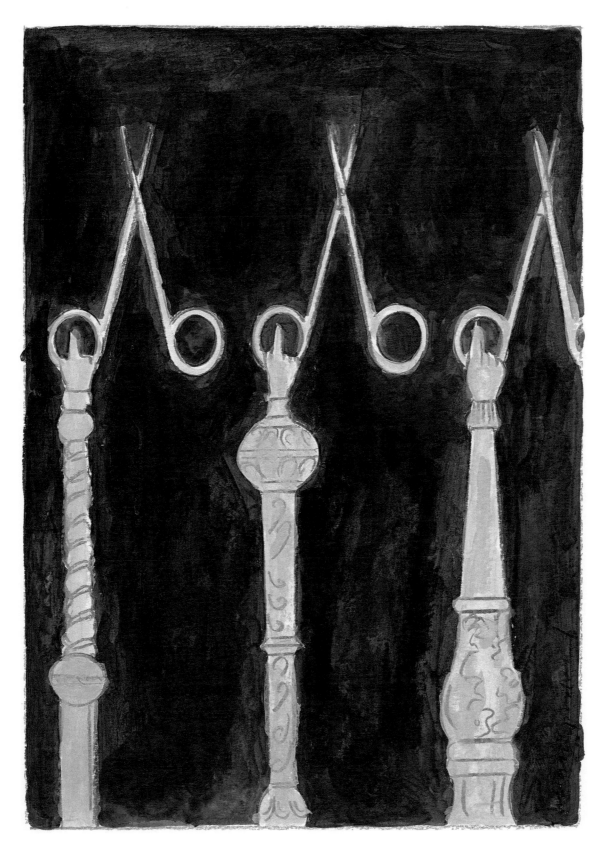

WILL BE SHORTLY CIRCUMCISED

Beide Rotten stehn schlagfertig	Either camp stands at the ready
Vor den Schranken in dem Saale,	To do battle in the hall,
Und das Volk mit Ungeduld	As the cheering gawkers wonder
Harret drängend der Signale.	Who will rise and who will fall.
Unterm güldnen Baldachin	Underneath a golden awning
Und umrauscht vom Hofgesinde	Sit the Spanish king and queen.
Sitzt der König und die Kön'gin;	She is girlish in her aspect,
Diese gleichet einem Kinde.	Seeming barely seventeen.
Ein französisch stumpfes Näschen,	She is delicate of feature,
Schalkheit kichert in den Mienen,	And her lips are ruby red.
Doch bezaubernd sind des Mundes	She seldom speaks her mind aloud,
Immer lächelnde Rubinen.	But she often laughs instead.
Schöne, flatterhafte Blume—	She's a lovely little flower,
Daß sich ihrer Gott erbarme—	From the lovely land of France.
Von dem heitern Seine-Ufer	May her God have mercy on her,
Wurde sie verpflanzt, die arme,	She's deserving of a chance.
Hierher in den steifen Boden	She was once called Blanche de Bourbon,
Der hispanischen Grandezza;	But is Donna Blanca now.
Weiland hieß sie Blanch' de Bourbon,	May she never know of troubles
Donna Blanka heißt sie jetzo.	That might line her lovely brow.
Pedro wird genannt der König,	Cruel Pedro is her husband.
Mit dem Zusatz der Grausame;	Some say he's a heartless swine,
Aber heute, milden Sinnes,	But today his mood is genial,
Ist er besser als sein Name.	And in fact, he feels benign.
Unterhält sich gut gelaunt	Now he banters with his nobles,
Mit des Hofes Edelleuten;	Feeling thoroughly at ease,
Auch den Juden und den Mohren	And with Moors and Jews exchanges
Sagt er viele Artigkeiten.	Many idle pleasantries.

60

70

80

CRUEL PEDRO

Diese Ritter ohne Vorhaut	They are knights devoid of foreskins,
Sind des Königs Lieblingsschranzen,	These factotums he adores.
Sie befehl'gen seine Heere,	Many oversee his coffers,
Sie verwalten die Finanzen.	Others fight his bloody wars.
Aber plötzlich Paukenschläge,	Now the booming sound of drumbeats
Und es melden die Trompeten,	Fills the monumental space,
Daß begonnen hat der Maulkampf,	As the Capuchin and rabbi
Der Disput der zwey Athlethen.	Stand there glaring, face to face.
Der Gardian der Franziskaner	The defender of the Christians
Bricht hervor mit frommem Grimme;	Issues forth with pious rage.
Polternd roh und widrig greinend	And with voice, both rough and whining,
Ist abwechselnd seine Stimme.	Wholly dominates the stage.
In des Vaters und des Sohnes	He invokes his mighty Father,
Und des heil'gen Geistes Namen	Sacred Son, and Holy Ghost,
Exorziret er den Rabbi,	Screaming "Jews are often devils,
Jakobs maledeiten Samen.	That is why we hate them most.
Denn bey solchen Controversen	"Jews are nasty little creatures,
Sind oft Teufelchen verborgen	Jews are Jacob's cursed seed,
In dem Juden, die mit Scharfsinn,	Stocked with wittiness and logic
Witz und Gründen ihn versorgen.	No one ever seems to need.
Nun die Teufel ausgetrieben	"Now I exorcise your demon,
Durch die Macht des Exorzismus,	Now I drive your evil out,
Kommt der Mönch auch zur Dogmatik,	Now it's time for Christian dogma,
Kugelt ab den Katechismus.	About which I have no doubt.
Er erzählt, daß in der Gottheit	"It informs us that our Godhead,
Drei Personen sind enthalten,	So exquisitely sublime,
Die jedoch zu einer einz'gen,	Has three different people in it,
Wenn es passend, sich gestalten—	And just one at the same time.

Line numbers in right margin: 90 (at "Issues forth with pious rage."), 100 (at "No one ever seems to need.")

Ein Mysterium, das nur	"It's a mystery that's fathomed
Von demjen'gen wird verstanden,	By the fortunate whose brains 110
Der entsprungen ist dem Kerker	Are not prisoners of reason
Der Vernunft und ihren Banden.	And the torment of its chains.
Er erzählt: wie Gott der Herr	"It tells of how dear Jesus
Ward zu Bethlehem geboren	Came to life in poverty
Von der Jungfrau, welche niemals	As the Son of blessed Mary,
Ihre Jungferschaft verloren;	Who retained her purity.
Wie der Herr der Welt gelegen	"It reminds us how our Savior,
In der Krippe, und ein Kühlein	In a manger cold and dim,
Und ein Oechslein bei ihm stunden,	Lay upon the straw serenely
Schier andächtig, zwey Rindviehlein.	As the cattle gazed at Him. 120
Er erzählte: wie der Herr	"And it tells how Herod's henchmen,
Vor den Schergen des Herodes	Evil ministers of death,
Nach Egypten floh, und später	First pursued then tortured Jesus
Litt die herbe Pein des Todes	Till He drew His final breath.
Unter Pontio Pilato,	"And it tells how Pontius Pilate,
Der das Urtheil unterschrieben,	Urged by Jews and other dross,
Von den harten Pharisäern,	Signed the catastrophic judgment
Von den Juden angetrieben.	That sent Jesus to the cross.
Er erzählte: wie der Herr,	"And it tells of how our Savior,
Der entstiegen seinem Grabe	Newly risen from His grave, 130
Schon am dritten Tag, gen Himmel	Took to wing and flew to heaven,
Seinen Flug genommen habe;	Where His killers He forgave.
Wie er aber, wenn es Zeit ist,	"And how, upon the end of days
Wiederkehren auf die Erde	He will come to Earth again,
Und zu Josaphat die Todten	And at Josaphat pass judgment
Und Lebend'gen richten werde.	On all dead and living men.

»Zittert, Juden!« rief der Mönch,	"Tremble, Jews," the monk exhorted,
»Vor dem Gott, den Ihr mit Hieben	"Bow before the god you beat,
Und mit Dornen habt gemartert	that you brutalized and martyred,
Den Ihr in den Tod getrieben.	for you soon will face defeat. 140
Seine Mörder, Volk der Rachsucht,	"You are foul, vindictive people,
Juden, das seyd ihr gewesen—	Each and every single Jew.
Immer meuchelt Ihr den Heiland,	You assassinate the Savior
Welcher kommt, Euch zu erlösen.	Who has come to rescue you.
Judenvolk, du bist ein Aas,	"You are little more than carrion,
Worin hausen die Dämonen;	Your bodies are a hell,
Eure Leiber sind Kasernen	A grotesque accommodation
Für des Teufels Legionen.	Where uncounted devils dwell.
Thomas von Aquino sagt es,	"Thus observes Thomas Aquinas,
Den man nennt den großen Ochsen	Often known as 'the great ox,' 150
Der Gelehrsamkeit, er ist	Of the sort of erudition
Licht und Lust der Orthodoxen.	Loved by Christian orthodox.
Judenvolk, Ihr seyd Hyänen,	"Jewish people, you are jackals,
Wölfe, Schakals, die in Gräbern	Wolves, hyenas, mired in mud,
Wühlen, um der Todten Leichnam'	Running roughshod over corpses
Blutfraßgierig aufzustöbern.	In your greedy thirst for blood.
Juden, Juden, Ihr seyd Säue,	"You are crocodiles and vampires,
Paviane, Nashornthiere,	Filthy monkeys, foul baboons,
Die man nennt Rhinozerosse,	You are swine and grimy werewolves
Crokodile und Vampyre.	Vainly baying at the moon. 160
Ihr seyd Raben, Eulen, Uhus,	"You are vultures, you are vermin,
Fledermäuse, Wiedehöpfe,	You are basilisks and bats,
Leichenhühner, Basilisken,	Packs of nauseating creatures,
Galgenvögel, Nachtgeschöpfe.	Brutish rhinos, loathsome rats.

Ihr seyd Vipern und Blindschleichen,
Klapperschlangen, gift'ge Kröten,
Ottern, Nattern—Christus wird
Eur verfluchtes Haupt zertreten.

Oder wollt Ihr, Maledeiten,
Eure armen Seelen retten?
Aus der Bosheit Synagoge
Flüchtet nach den frommen Stätten,

Nach der Liebe lichtem Dome,
Wo im benedeiten Becken
Euch der Quell der Gnade sprudelt—
Drin sollt Ihr die Köpfe stecken—

Wascht dort ab den alten Adam
Und die Laster, die ihn schwärzen;
Des verjährten Grolles Schimmel,
Wascht ihn ab von Euren Herzen!

Hört Ihr nicht des Heilands Stimme?
Euren neuen Namen rief er—
Lauset Euch an Christi Brust
Von der Sünde Ungeziefer!

Unser Gott, der ist die Liebe,
Und er gleichet einem Lamme;
Um zu sühnen unsre Schuld
Starb er an des Kreuzes Stamme.

Unser Gott, der ist die Liebe,
Jesus Christus ist sein Namen;
Seine Duldsamkeit und Demuth
Suchen wir stets nachzuahmen.

"You are horrible to look at,
Things with ghastly horns and snouts.
You are frightful poison vipers
Slowly slithering about.

"Save your souls, unhappy wretches,
Poison toads, disgusting hogs.   170
Leave your miserable religion,
Flee your evil synagogues.

"Gather in our sacred churches,
It's the wisest thing to do.
Join us and our blessed Savior,
Let His love flow over you.

"Wash away the sins of Adam,
Wash away the ancient wrath.
Fill your hearts with Christian goodness,
You will find no better path.   180

"Can you hear our Savior calling?
He is uttering your name.
Now embrace our God almighty,
And eliminate your shame.

"Our dear God is love eternal
And His name is Jesus Christ.
In the hope that He might save us,
His own life He sacrificed.

"Our true God is like no other,
Gentle as a lamb is He,   190
Teaching us the ways of kindness,
Caring, love, humility.

HIS OWN LIFE HE SACRIFICED

GENTLE AS A LAMB IS HE

Deßhalb sind wir auch so sanft,
So leutselig, ruhig, milde,
Hadern niemals, nach des Lammes,
Des Versöhners, Musterbilde.

Einst im Himmel werden wir
Ganz verklärt zu frommen Englein,
Und wir wandeln dort gottselig,
In den Händen Lilienstenglein.

Statt der groben Kutten tragen
Wir die reinlichsten Gewänder
Von Moußlin, Brokat und Seide,
Goldne Troddeln, bunte Bänder.

Keine Glatze mehr! Goldlocken
Flattern dort um unsre Köpfe;
Allerliebste Jungfraun flechten
Uns das Haar in hübsche Zöpfe.

Weinpokale wird es droben
Von viel weiterm Umfang geben,
Als die Becher sind hier unten,
Worin schäumt der Saft der Reben.

Doch im Gegentheil viel enger
Als ein Weibermund hienieden,
Wird das Frauenmündchen seyn,
Das dort oben uns beschieden.

Trinkend, küssend, lachend wollen
Wir die Ewigkeit verbringen,
Und verzückt Halleluja,
Kyrie Eleyson singen.«

"This is why we are as docile
    As a sweet and sinless child,
    Why we never carp or quarrel,
    Why we're affable and mild.

"This is why we'll go to heaven,
    Holding lilies in our hands,
    Why, transformed to blessed angels,
    We will join the angel band.   200

"We will wear the purest garments,
    Soft as satin, white as milk,
    Fringed with multicolored ribbons,
    Tassels of the finest silk.

"Golden locks, long and resplendent,
    Surely will bedeck us there,
    While the loveliest of maidens
    Gently braid our flowing hair.

"And the wines will be much finer
    Than the wines that we now know,   210
    And the goblets will be larger
    Than the goblets here below.

"But the mouth of every woman
    Will be smaller up above,
    Never shouting out in anger,
    Only speaking words of love.

"There we'll sing loud hallelujahs,
    There we'll drink and laugh and kiss,
    There we'll dance in endless rapture,
    And profound eternal bliss."   220

Also schloß der Christ. Die Mönchlein
Glaubten schon, Erleuchtung träte
In die Herzen, und sie schleppten
Flink herbey das Taufgeräthe.

Doch die wasserscheuen Juden
Schütteln sich und grinsen schnöde.
Rabbi Juda, der Navarrer,
Hub jetzt an die Gegenrede:

»Um für deine Saat zu düngen
Meines Geistes dürren Acker,
Mit Mistkarren voll Schimpfwörter
Hast du mich beschmissen wacker.

So folgt jeder der Methode,
Dran er nun einmal gewöhnet,
Und anstatt dich drob zu schelten,
Sag' ich Dank dir, wohlversöhnet.

Die Dreyeinigkeitsdoktrin
Kann für unsre Leut nicht passen,
Die mit Regula-de-tri
Sich von Jugend auf befassen.

Daß in deinem Gotte drey,
Drey Personen sind enthalten
Ist bescheiden noch, sechstausend
Götter gab es bey den Alten.

Unbekannt ist mir der Gott,
Den Ihr Christum pflegt zu nennen;
Seine Jungfer Mutter gleichfalls
Hab ich nicht die Ehr zu kennen.

Thus the Capuchin concluded,
And his men seemed overjoyed,
Thinking that the rabbi's viewpoint
Had already been destroyed.

But the Jews, not fond of water,
Merely looked with unconcern
As Rabbi Judah cleared his throat
Then said, "Now it is my turn.

"Though you spoke of peace and goodness,
Nonetheless, with bitter tongue,   230
You assaulted me with insults,
And you pummeled me with dung.

"Each religion has its method
And its parliamentary laws.
If your method serves you justly,
I will give you my applause.

"But we Jews don't share your doctrine
Of a holy trinity.
It is far too inconsistent
With our ideology.   240

"Our beliefs are so divergent
That we'll always be at odds.
By the way, the foolish ancients
Had at least six thousand gods.

"I have never met your Jesus,
Who, I've heard, endured much strife,
And I do not know the Virgin
Who allowed Him earthly life.

AND YOU PUMMELED ME WITH DUNG

Ich bedaure, daß er einst,	"I am sorry that your Savior,
Vor etwa zwölfhundert Jahren,	All those centuries ago
Ein'ge Unannehmlichkeiten	In Jerusalem had troubles
Zu Jerusalem erfahren.	That would sadly lay Him low.
Ob die Juden ihn getödtet,	"Was it Jews who slew your Savior
Das ist schwer jetzt zu erkunden,	In a mob that shrieked and jeered?
Da ja das Corpus Delicti	The reports are inconclusive,
Schon am dritten Tag verschwunden.	For His corpse soon disappeared.
Daß er ein Verwandter sey	"Is your God akin to our God?
Unsres Gottes, ist nicht minder	Such a notion is absurd,
Zweifelhaft; so viel wir wissen	For our God has had no children,
Hat der letzte keine Kinder.	None of whom, at least, we've heard.
Unser Gott ist nicht gestorben	"Our God has never perished,
Als ein armes Lämmerschwänzchen	He continues to exist.
Für die Menschheit, ist kein süßes	Our God is not a tender lamb,
Philantröpfchen, Faselhänschen.	Or sweet philanthropist.
Unser Gott ist nicht die Liebe;	"Our God is not a dulcet bird,
Schnäbeln ist nicht seine Sache,	He does not sweetly sing.
Denn er ist ein Donnergott	He is a vengeful thunder god
Und er ist ein Gott der Rache.	Who makes the mountains ring.
Seines Zornes Blitze treffen	"He turns His wrath on sinners,
Unerbittlich jeden Sünder,	Rarely stopping to forewarn.
Und des Vaters Schulden büßen	He strikes the sinners' children,
Oft die späten Enkelkinder.	Even those as yet unborn.
Unser Gott, der ist lebendig	"Our God has boundless power,
Und in seiner Himmelshalle	And, immune to all disease,
Existiret er drauf los	He rules over all existence
Durch die Ewigkeiten alle.	And through all eternities.

Line numbers in right margin: 250, 260, 270

Unser Gott, und der ist auch
Ein gesunder Gott, kein Mythos
Bleich und dünne wie Oblaten
Oder Schatten am Cocythos.

Unser Gott ist stark. In Händen
Trägt er Sonne, Mond, Gestirne;
Throne brechen, Völker schwinden,
Wenn er runzelt seine Stirne.

Und er ist ein großer Gott.
David singt: Ermessen ließe
Sich die Größe nicht, die Erde
Sei der Schemel seiner Füße.

Unser Gott liebt die Musik,
Saitenspiel und Festgesänge;
Doch wie Ferkelgrunzen sind
Ihm zuwider Glockenklänge.

Leviathan heißt der Fisch,
Welcher haust im Meeresgrunde;
Mit ihm spielet Gott der Herr
Alle Tage eine Stunde—

Ausgenommen an dem neunten
Tag des Monats Ab, wo nämlich
Eingeäschert ward sein Tempel;
An dem Tag ist er zu grämlich.

Des Leviathan's Länge ist
Hundert Meilen, hat Floßfedern
Groß wie König Ok von Basan,
Und sein Schwanz ist wie ein Cedern.

"Our God is not some simple myth,
  Our God is everywhere.
  No matter where you turn your eyes,
  You'll find Him always there.   280

"Our God is so magnificent,
  His scope and reach so vast,
  He holds the very stars in place.
  His strength is unsurpassed.

"Indeed, He is omnipotent,
  So hallowed are His ways.
  He is past all earthly measure
  And deserves our highest praise.

"Although our God loves music
  And thinks singing is divine,   290
  He compares the sound of church bells
  To the ugly grunts of swine.

"A massive fish, Leviathan,
  Dwells near the ocean floor.
  Our God plays with it daily
  For an hour, maybe more.

"Except upon the ninth of Av,
  For on that joyless day
  His temple was consumed by flames—
  He's too morose to play.   300

"There's no fish like Leviathan,
  A hundred miles in length.
  Its tail and fins are massive things,
  It has tremendous strength.

OUR GOD LOVES MUSIC

Doch sein Fleisch ist delikat,
Delikater als Schildkröten,
Und am Tag der Auferstehung
Wird der Herr zu Tische beten

Alle frommen Auserwählten,
Die Gerechten und die Weisen—
Unsres Herrgotts Lieblingsfisch
Werden sie alsdann verspeisen,

Theils mit weißer Knoblauchbrühe,
Theils auch braun in Wein gesotten,
Mit Gewürzen und Rosinen,
Ungefähr wie Matelotten.

In der weißen Knoblauchbrühe
Schwimmen kleine Schäbchen Rettig—
So bereitet, Frater Jose,
Mundet dir das Fischlein, wett' ich!

Auch die braune ist so lecker,
Nemlich die Rosinensauce,
Sie wird himmlisch wohl behagen
Deinem Bäuchlein, Frater Jose.

Was Gott kocht, ist gut gekocht!
Mönchlein, nimm jetzt meinen Rath an,
Opfre hin die alte Vorhaut
Und erquick' dich am Leviathan.«

Also lockend sprach der Rabbi,
Lockend, ködernd, heimlich schmunzelnd,
Und die Juden schwangen schon
Ihre Messer wonnegrunzelnd,

"And yet its flesh is delicate,
Its flavor mild and sweet.
There's never been a finer fish
That one could hope to eat.

"On the day of resurrection
God will pick a pious few   310
To dine upon Leviathan,
Which they will gladly do.

"Partly simmered in brown gravy,
Partly steeped in garlic sauce,
The result will be so wondrous,
None will need a second course.

"Wispy ribbons of horseradish
Will adorn this flawless dish.
I can't envisage, Don José,
You could resist this fish.   320

"The flavors, so exquisite,
So superb in every way,
Would impart the utmost pleasure
To your belly, Don José.

"Perhaps you'll taste this wondrous fish
If you take my advice
And remove your useless foreskin,
It's a minor sacrifice."

Thus concluded Rabbi Judah
Smiling secretly inside   330
As his men, in sheer elation,
Waved their shining knives with pride.

Um als Sieger zu skalpiren
Die verfallenen Vorhäute,
Wahre *spolia opima*
In dem wunderlichen Streite.

Doch die Mönche hielten fest
An dem väterlichen Glauben
Und an ihrer Vorhaut, ließen
Sich derselben nicht berauben.

Nach dem Juden sprach aufs neue
Der katholische Bekehrer;
Wieder schimpft er, jedes Wort
Ist ein Nachttopf, und kein leerer.

Darauf replizirt der Rabbi
Mit zurückgehaltnem Eifer;
Wie sein Herz auch überkocht,
Doch verschluckt er seinen Geifer.

Er beruft sich auf die Mischna,
Commentare und Traktate;
Bringt auch aus dem Tausves-Jontof
Viel beweisende Citate.

Aber welche Blasphemie
Mußt' er von dem Mönche hören!
Dieser sprach: der Tausves-Jontof
Möge sich zum Teufel scheren.

»Da hört alles auf, o Gott!«
Kreischt der Rabbi jetzt entsetzlich;
Und es reißt ihm die Geduld;
Rappelköpfig wird er plötzlich.

They believed their side had triumphed,
That the monks would now concede
And foreswear their wrinkled foreskins,
Things they truly did not need.

But the monks were far from ready
To renounce these artifacts,
Convinced their blessed faith would keep
Their nether parts intact.   340

The Capuchin then spoke again,
His voice was harsh and hot.
His horrid words belonged inside
A filthy chamber pot.

The rabbi cried with righteous ire
He could not quite conceal.
His bitter bile arose,
He almost vomited his meal.

He called upon the Mishna,
Citing many proofs and quotes,   350
Plus the trusted Tausves-Yontof
With its endless anecdotes.

 The monk retorted viciously,
 "Be damned," he wildly yelled.
 "May your precious Tausves-Yontof
 And yourself go straight to hell."

"You've gone too far," the rabbi shrieks,
 His face contorts with pain.
 His patience is exhausted,
 He is practically insane.   360

»Gilt nichts mehr der Tausves-Jontof,
Was soll gelten? Zeter! Zeter!
Räche, Herr, die Missethat,
Strafe, Herr, den Uebelthäter!

Denn der Tausves-Jontof, Gott,
Das bist du! Und an dem frechen
Tausvesjontof-Läugner mußt du
Deines Namens Ehre rächen.

Laß den Abgrund ihn verschlingen,
Wie des Kora böse Rotte,
Die sich wider dich empört
Durch Emeute und Complotte.

Donnre deinen besten Donner!
Strafe, o mein Gott, den Frevel—
Hattest du doch zu Sodoma
Und Gomorrha Pech und Schwefel!

Treffe, Herr, die Kapuziner,
Wie du Pharaon getroffen,
Der uns nachgesetzt, als wir
Wohl bepackt davon geloffen.

Hunderttausend Ritter folgten
Diesem König von Mizrayim,
Stahlbepanzert, blanke Schwerter
In den schrecklichen Jadayim.

Gott! da hast du ausgestreckt
Deine Jad, und sammt dem Heere
Ward ertränkt, wie junge Katzen,
Pharao im rothen Meere.

"This fundamental insult is
 Not one I will soon forget.
 You have dared malign a holy
 Tome that's not been written yet.

"To deny the Tausves-Yontof
 Is to disavow and shun
 The Ruler of the universe—
 Take vengeance, mighty One.

"Let him who would deny You
 Plunge into the great Abyss,   370
 Like Korah's vile conspirators,
 Whom nobody seems to miss.

"Strike him down with thunderbolts,
 Destroy this dreadful man,
 Almighty One who's ruled the Earth
 Since time itself began.

"As once You struck down Pharaoh,
 To avenge his every sin,
 Reach out Your hand, annihilate
 This wicked Capuchin.   380

"How easily You once destroyed
 Dread Pharaoh's valiant knights,
 And effortlessly blotted out
 The evil Sodomites.

"You swatted Pharaoh's army
 As a man might swat a flea,
 And every soldier perished
 At the bottom of the sea.

Treffe, Herr, die Kapuziner,
Zeige den infamen Schuften,
Daß die Blitze deines Zorns
Nicht verrauchten und verpufften.

Deines Sieges Ruhm und Preis
Will ich singen dann und sagen,
Und dabey, wie Mirjam that
Tanzen und die Pauke schlagen.«

In die Rede grimmig fiel
Jetzt der Mönch dem Zornentflammten:
»Mag dich selbst der Herr verderben,
Dich Verfluchten und Verdammten!

Trotzen kann ich deinen Teufeln,
Deinem schmutz'gen Fliegengotte,
Luzifer und Belzebube
Belial und Astarothe.

Trotzen kann ich deinen Geistern,
Deinen dunkeln Höllenpossen,
Denn in mir ist Jesus Christus,
Habe seinen Leib genossen.

Christus ist mein Leibgericht,
Schmeckt viel besser als Leviathan
Mit der weißen Knoblauchsauce,
Die vielleicht gekocht der Satan.

Ach! anstatt zu disputiren,
Lieber möcht' ich schmoren, braten
Auf dem wärmsten Scheiterhaufen
Dich und deine Kameraden.«

"Strike now, great Lord, this Capuchin,
    Perhaps he then may learn   390
    That the furnace of Your anger
    Still interminably burns.

"Then I will dance for days and days,
    And I will beat the drum,
    And I will sing in praise of You
    Until my throat goes numb."

The monk, consumed with righteous rage,
    Malevolently cursed.
"Be damned, horrendous Hebrew.
    Wretched rabbi, you're the worst.   400

"I defy your worthless devils,
    Lucifer and Beelzebub.
    Your Belial and Ashtoreth
    Are little more than grubs.

"I defy your putrid spirits,
    Demons from a thousand hells,
    For I am suffused with Jesus,
    Deep within me He now dwells.

"Christ is my quintessential food,
    And furthermore, I say   410
    Perhaps it's Satan that will cook
    Leviathan one day.

"Instead of just debating,
    For there is no sense to it,
    I would roast you and your comrades
    Very slowly, on a spit."

Also tos't in Schimpf und Ernst	Thus with escalating insults
Das Turney für Gott und Glauben,	The relentless contest raged.
Doch die Kämpen ganz vergeblich	Neither man made any headway
Kreischen, schelten, wüthen, schnauben.	In the pointless war they waged. 420
Schon zwölf Stunden währt der Kampf,	They disputed for twelve hours
Dem kein End ist abzuschauen;	Without any end in sight.
Müde wird das Publikum	Many people started yawning
Und es schwitzen stark die Frauen.	As day slowly turned to night.
Auch der Hof wird ungeduldig,	They were clearly losing interest
Manche Zofe gähnt ein wenig.	In this unproductive scene,
Zu der schönen Königin	So the King, inclined to end it,
Wendet fragend sich der König:	Now inquired of the Queen—
Sagt mir, was ist Eure Meinung?	"In your very best opinion
Wer hat Recht von diesen beiden?	Which of them should now prevail? 430
Wollt Ihr für den Rabbi Euch	Is it Capuchin or rabbi?
Oder für den Mönch entscheiden?	Who should triumph? Who should fail?"
Donna Blanka schaut ihn an	Donna Blanca giggled nervously,
Und wie sinnend ihre Hände	Not being well-designed
Mit verschränkten Fingern drückt sie	To explore the inner workings
An die Stirn und spricht am Ende:	Of her adolescent mind.
Welcher Recht hat, weiß ich nicht—	She chirped, "I cannot imagine,
Doch es will mich schier bedünken,	But there's one thing that I think—
Daß der Rabbi und der Mönch,	Both this Capuchin and rabbi
Daß sie alle beide stinken.	Most insufferably stink." 440

—TRANSLATED BY JACK PRELUTSKY

THEY DISPUTED FOR TWELVE HOURS

[QUEEN] DONNA BLANCA

Notes

*The notes below are keyed to the line numbers
of each poem.*

Princess Sabbath

1 *Arabia's book of legends*: The Thousand and One Nights.

31 *Tents of Jacob*: "How goodly are thy tents, O Jacob, and thy tabernacles, O Israel!" (Numbers 24:5 KJV).

32 *I now kiss your holy doorposts*: The mezuzah is a parchment scroll inscribed on one side with the biblical passages Deuteronomy 6:4 and 11:13–21 and on the other side with the divine name Shaddai, inserted in a small tube and attached by many Jews to the doorposts of their homes. The custom is to touch it upon entering a house and to kiss the finger that touched it.

44 *bimah*: The raised platform around the sanctuary.

68 *Yehuda ben Halévi*: The poet's name was Yehuda Halevi (ca. 1075–1141); "ben" (son of) is Heine's quirky, incorrect addition. His Hebrew was poor, and besides, he needed an extra syllable here for the meter. The Sabbath poem (*Lekhá dodí* in the Sephardic pronunciation) was actually written by the sixteenth-century mystic Shlomo Alkabetz.

75 *Queen of Sheba*: See 1 Kings 10:1–13.

100 *cholent*: A stewed or baked dish, especially of meat and beans, cooked the day before the Sabbath or overnight on a slow fire.

101–2 *Cholent, light direct from heaven, / Daughter of Elysium!*: A parody of the beginning of Schiller's "Ode to Joy," the text for the fourth movement of Beethoven's Ninth Symphony.

141–52 *Princess Sabbath . . . goes out*: Heine is referring to the ceremony of Havdalah, performed by observant Jews at the conclusion of the Sabbath; it consists of blessings over wine, spices, and the light of a candle. —S. M.

Yehuda ben Halévi

1–4 *If I ever should forget thee*: A paraphrase of Psalm 137:5–6.

26–27 *seven hundred fifty / Years*: According to Heine's source, Yehuda Halevi was born in 1105.

29 *Toledo*: He was actually born in Tudela.

47 *trope*: The ritual chanting used for the reading of the Torah.

52 *shalshélet*: One of the rarest cantillation marks, occurring just four times in the whole Torah. It is rendered musically by a long and elaborate string of notes, giving a strong emphasis to the word it marks.

53 *Targum Onkelos*: A famous Aramaic paraphrase of the Bible. Its authorship is traditionally attributed to the Roman convert Onkelos (ca. 35–110 CE).

55 *Antique Jewish dialect*: Aramaic is actually a separate but cognate language. It replaced Hebrew as the principal spoken language of the Jews after the Babylonian exile (597–539 BCE).

59 *Swabian*: The dialect of Swabia, in southwest Germany; it is difficult for speakers of standard German to understand.

68 *halákha* (*halakhá* in the Sephardic pronunciation): The traditional Jewish law, the parts of the Talmud dedicated to laws and legal interpretation.

71 *Pumbedita*: City in ancient Babylon, famous for its Talmudic academy.

76 *Kuzari*: Yehuda Halevi's most famous prose work, a book of apologetics completed around 1140.

85 *aggádah* (*aggadáh* in the Sephardic pronunciation): A collection of rabbinic texts, particularly in the Talmud and Midrash, that comprises folklore, history, or pseudohistory, ethics, and practical advice.

91 *Semíramis*: The Assyrian queen Shammuramat, wife of Shamshi-Adad V. After her husband's death, she served as regent for her son from 811 to 806 BCE According to legend, she was abandoned by her parents, and doves fed her until Simmas, the royal shepherd, found and raised her. The Hanging Gardens of Babylon were attributed to her by some ancient historians.

92 *eighth wonder*: On the classic lists of the seven wonders of the world, the Hanging Gardens were number three.

124 *Egg the hen laid on a feast day*: For Heine the dispute about whether an egg laid on the Sabbath should be eaten is an example of the triviality of Talmudic quibbling.

160 *the wilderness of exile*: The exile began after the destruction of Jerusalem in 70 CE and lasted until after Heine's death.

181 *By the streams of Babylon*: "By the rivers of Babylon, there we sat down, yea, we wept, when we remembered Zion.

We hanged our harps upon the willows in the midst
thereof" (Psalm 137:1–2 KJV).

182 *Zion*: The oldest part of Jerusalem. It is often equivalent to
Jerusalem or the whole land of Israel.

192 *Job's pustules*: In Job there are boils but no dog. Heine
confused Job with the beggar Lazarus in Luke 16:20–21:
"And there was a certain beggar named Lazarus, which was
laid at his gate, full of sores, and desiring to be fed with the
crumbs which fell from the rich man's table: moreover the
dogs came and licked his sores" (KJV).

206 *Happy shall he be*: "O daughter of Babylon, who art to be
destroyed; happy shall he be, that rewardeth thee as thou
hast served us. Happy shall he be, that taketh and dasheth
thy little ones against the stones" (Psalm 137:8–9 KJV).

213 *wingèd horse*: Pegasus.

261 *Laura*: On April 6, 1327, the sight of a woman named Laura,
in the church of Sainte-Claire d'Avignon, kindled in the
poet Francesco Petrarca (Petrarch) an enduring passion,
which he celebrated in *Rime sparse* (Scattered rhymes).

270 *Court of Love*: There were actual Courts of Love in France,
beginning in the twelfth century, presided over by famous
noblewomen, in which questions about love—for example,
"Is love possible between married spouses?"—were argued
and decided.

275 *destruction*: Jerusalem was destroyed in 70 CE by the future
emperor Titus.

323 *Ninth day of the month of Av*: The ninth of Av (in Hebrew,
Tisha b'Av) is an annual fast day that commemorates the
anniversary of a number of disasters in Jewish history,
primarily the destruction of both the First Temple by the
Babylonians in 587 BCE and the Second Temple by the
Romans in 70 CE

337 *Jaufré Rudel*: Prince of Blaye and a troubadour, born
between 1110 and 1130, died, according to legend, ca. 1148,
during the Second Crusade, or later ca. 1170.

350 *Cette (now Sète)*: A port on the Mediterranean, in the
former province of Languedoc, birthplace of Paul Valéry.

366–67 *At the feet of his belovèd / Died*: Yehuda Halevi died about
1141, shortly after arriving in Israel.

369 *Arbéla*: The Battle of Arbela in 331 BCE was the decisive
battle of Alexander the Great's invasion of the Persian
Achaemenid Empire.

371 *Daríus*: Darius III (ca. 380–330 BCE), the last king of the
Achaemenid Empire.

395 *Cyrus*: Cyrus the Great (ca. 600–530 BCE), the founder of
the Achaemenid Empire, who created the largest empire
the world had ever seen.

398 *bottom-thwacker*: Aristotle tutored Alexander until he was
sixteen. Heine imagines him as a schoolmaster who thumps
learning into the backsides of his pupils. (In "Among School

Children," Yeats imagines him in the same way: "Solider
Aristotle played the taws / Upon the bottom of a king of
kings.")

403 *Smerdis*: A son of Cyrus the Great and younger brother
of Cambyses II. After his brother had him secretly put to
death, an imposter pretending to be Smerdis appeared
in 522 and proclaimed himself king. Because the people
hated Cambyses for his despotism, they acknowledged
the imposter as king, and he ruled over the empire for
seven months. But then a group of seven nobles, having
discovered his secret, stabbed him to death. One of the
seven, Darius, was proclaimed as king.

404 *Atossa (550–475 BCE)*: Daughter of Cyrus the Great, sister
of Cambyses II. She married Darius I in 522 after he had
defeated the followers of the false Smerdis.

408 *Thaïs*: A famous Greek courtesan who accompanied
Alexander the Great on his campaigns. According to
Plutarch, at a party in Persepolis, she gave a speech that
convinced Alexander to burn the palace in revenge for the
destruction of Athens.

425 *Cleopatra*: "There were formerly two pearls, the largest
that had been ever seen in the whole world: Cleopatra,
the last of the queens of Egypt, was in possession of them
both, they having come to her by descent from the kings
of the East. When Antony had been sated by her, day
after day, with the most exquisite banquets, this queenly
courtesan, inflated with vanity and disdainful arrogance,
affected to treat all this sumptuousness and all these vast
preparations with the greatest contempt; upon which
Antony enquired what there was that could possibly be
added to such extraordinary magnificence. To this she
made answer, that on a single entertainment she would
expend ten millions of sesterces. Antony was extremely
desirous to learn how that could be done, but looked
upon it as a thing quite impossible; and a wager was the
result. On the following day, upon which the matter was
to be decided, in order that she might not lose the wager,
she had an entertainment set before Antony, magnificent
in every respect, though no better than his usual repast.
Upon this, Antony joked her, and enquired what was the
amount expended upon it; to which she made answer
that the banquet which he then beheld was only a trifling
appendage to the real banquet, and that she alone would
consume at the meal to the ascertained value of that
amount, she herself would swallow the ten millions of
sesterces; and so ordered the second course to be served.
In obedience to her instructions, the servants placed before
her a single vessel, which was filled with vinegar, a liquid
the sharpness and strength of which is able to dissolve
pearls. At this moment she was wearing in her ears those

choicest and most rare and unique productions of nature; and while Antony was waiting to see what she was going to do, taking one of them from out of her ear, she threw it into the vinegar, and as soon as it was melted, she swallowed it." (Pliny the Elder, *Natural History* 9.58; John Bostock, trans., *The Natural History of Pliny*, vol. 2 [London: Henry G. Bohn, 1855].)

429–30 *After the Omáyyads conquered / Spain*: From 711 to 788.

433 *Ábderam the Third*: Abd ar-Rahman ibn Muhammad (891–961), also known as Abd-Rahman III, was the eighth independent emir and first Omayyad caliph of Cordoba (929–61). During his reign, Cordoba became the most important intellectual center of Western Europe.

445 *autos-da-fé*: An auto-da-fé was the ritual of public penance from condemned heretics and apostates during the Spanish and Portuguese Inquisitions. The harshest punishment imposed was burning at the stake.

449 *Mendizábal*: Juan Álvarez Mendizábal (1790–1853), liberal Spanish economist and politician who served as third Prime Minister of Spain. His mother was of Jewish descent. He was bitterly hated by Catholics for laws that resulted in the confiscation and sale of monastic properties in Spain.

456 *Baroness von Rothschild*: Betty de Rothschild (1805–1886) was a friend of Heine's. She was married to the banker James Mayer de Rothschild, the founder of the French branch of the Rothschilds, and was one of the wealthiest women in Europe and a prominent Parisian patron of the arts. Her portrait by Ingres is considered one of his most accomplished works.

461 *he put the epics*: "When a small coffer was brought to him, which those in charge of the baggage and wealth of Darius thought the most precious thing there, he asked his friends what valuable object they thought would most fittingly be deposited in it. And when many answered and there were many opinions, Alexander himself said he was going to deposit the *Iliad* there for safe-keeping" (Plutarch, *Life of Alexander* 26; Bernadotte Perrin, trans., *Plutarch's Lives*, vol. 7, Loeb Classical Library 99 [London: William Heineman, 1919]).

479 *panthers*: Dionysus, god of wine, fertility, and religious ecstasy, is often depicted as standing in a chariot drawn by panthers.

484 *Crippled, and in anguish*: In May 1848, Heine was suddenly paralyzed and had to be confined to bed. He would not leave his "mattress-grave" until his death in 1856. *Hebrew Melodies* was published in 1851.

552 *Titus*: He destroyed Jerusalem in 70 CE Seven years later, after the death of his father, Vespasian, he became emperor.

573 *a savage Arab horseman*: The death of Yehuda Halevi at the hands of an Arab was a much-repeated legend.

631 *"Marquis"*: A famous Parisian chocolate shop.

632 *Le passage des Panoramas*: The oldest of the covered passageways in Paris, situated between the boulevard Montmartre and the rue Saint-Marc.

637 *Dearest child*: Heine was eighteen years older than his wife, Mathilde, whom he had met when she was nineteen.

659 *Solomon Gabírol* (1021/22–1058?): Solomon ibn Gabirol, known to Christians as Avicebron, Andalusian poet and philosopher.

660 *Moses ibn Ezra* (1055 or 1060–after 1138): Andalusian poet, linguist, and philosopher.

671 *Read, in the original*: Something Heine himself could not do, which makes the didactic tone here delicious. Heine's source for these poems, Michael Sachs's *Die religiöse Poesie der Juden in Spanien* (*The Religious Poetry of the Jews in Spain*) (Berlin: Beit, 1845), provided German translations of selected poems by Yehuda Halevi, Solomon ibn Gabirol, and Moses ibn Ezra.

677 *Al-Harízi*: Yehuda al-Harizi (1165–1225), Spanish rabbi, translator, poet, and traveler. He translated al-Hariri's *maqāmāt* (picaresque novellas, written mainly in rhymed prose) into Hebrew.

681 *Al-Haríri*: Abu Muhammad al-Qasim ibn Ali ibn Muhammad ibn Uthman al-Hariri (1054–1122), Arab poet, linguist, and high government official of the Seljuk Empire.

701 *Meyer*: Moses ibn Ezra had three brothers: Isaac, Joseph, and Judah, all of whom were distinguished scholars. After the arrival of the Almoravids, the Ibn Ezra family fortune was confiscated, and his three brothers had to flee.

703 *hopeless passion*: Ibn Ezra was rejected by his niece, who died shortly after marrying one of his brothers.

740 *shlemiel* (Yiddish): "In the common speech of the Jews, it refers to clumsy and unlucky people, who can't succeed at anything in the world. A shlemiel breaks his finger in his vest pocket; he falls on his back and breaks his nose" (Adelbert von Chamisso [see following note], in a letter to his brother Hippolyte).

746 *Chamisso*: Adelbert von Chamisso (1781–1838) made the word *shlemiel* famous through one of the most popular tales of the nineteenth century, *Peter Schlemihls Wundersame Geschichte* (*The Wonderful History of Peter Shlemiel*) (Nürnberg: Schrag, 1814); it was written to amuse the children of his friend Julius Eduard Hitzig (see note to line 758). In the story, Schlemihl sells his shadow to the Devil for a bottomless wallet, only to find that a man without a shadow is shunned by human society.

748 *Civil rights*: Though the word *shlemiel* had "civil rights," the Jews did not.

758 *Hitzig*: Julius Eduard Hitzig (1780–1849), friend and biographer of Adelbert von Chamisso. Born into the wealthy and influential Jewish Itzig family, he converted to Christianity in 1799 and changed his name to Hitzig in 1812. He was a Prussian civil servant between 1799 and 1806 and then became Criminal Counsel at the Berlin Supreme Court in 1815 and its director in 1825. In 1808, he established a publishing house and, later, a bookstore. Felix Mendelssohn was a cousin of his; other relatives were patrons of Mozart.

798 *Pinkhas*: "And one of the Israelite men came and brought into the camp a Midianite woman, in front of Moses and the whole community of Israel, while they were weeping at the entrance to the tent of meeting. And when Pinkhas, son of Eleazar, grandson of Aaron the priest, saw it, he stood up and left the assembly and took a spear in his hand, and he followed the Israelite into his tent and thrust his spear all the way though the man and the woman, through her belly. So the plague that had afflicted the Israelites was stopped" (Numbers 25:6–8). In the King James Version, the name is transliterated as Phinehas.

798 *Zimri*: "The name of the Israelite who was killed with the Midianite woman was Zimri, son of Salu, the leader of a family from the tribe of Simeon" (Numbers 25:14).

812 *Shlemiel ben Zurisháddai*: Shlumiel ben Zurishaddai (Numbers 1:6).

857 *Cordoba*: Gabirol actually died in Valencia. —S. M.

Disputation

11 *Capuchins*: An order of friars within the Catholic Church who wear brown robes with hoods (capuches). The order, founded in 1525, was inspired by the sentiment that the lifestyle led by the friars of the day was not the one abided by St. Francis of Assisi.

15 *Yarmulkes*: Brimless caps worn on the crown of the head by religious Jewish men (especially during prayer) as a reminder that God's presence is always above us. The word *yarmulke* comes from the Aramaic "yarei Malka"—to have "reverence for the King."

69 *Blanche de Bourbon* (1339–1361): Daughter of the Duke of Bourbon, and niece of John, king of France, betrothed at the age of fifteen to Don Pedro in 1352.

73 *Cruel Pedro* (1334–1369): King of Castile (1350–69) also known as "Pedro the Just." In 1353, Pedro secretly married Maria de Padilla, who would bear him four children. Later that year, Pedro was practically forced by his mother to marry Blanche de Bourbon and had to deny that a marriage with Maria ever took place. Almost immediately after the wedding to Blanche, Pedro deserted his new bride and returned to Maria.

121 *Herod* (20 BCE–39 CE): Ruler of Galilee (4–39 CE) who ordered the execution of John the Baptist and participated in the trial of Jesus.

125 *Pontius Pilate*: Governor of the Roman province of Judaea serving under Emperor Tiberius from 26/27 to 36/37 CE According to the Gospels, Pilate presided over the trial and crucifixion of Jesus.

135 *Josaphat*: Valley located between the walled old city of Jerusalem and the Mount of Olives, where it is said the events of Judgment Day will take place (Joel 3:12) and all nations will be judged.

149 *Thomas Aquinas* (1224–1274): A Dominican friar and priest notable as a scholastic theologian and philosopher honored as a saint and Doctor of the Church. As Thomas was quiet and rarely spoke, some of his fellow students thought he was slow. Dominican scholar Albertus Magnus, however, prophetically exclaimed, "You call him the dumb ox, but in his teaching he will one day produce such a bellowing that it will be heard throughout the world."

293 *Leviathan*: According to Jewish tradition, the Leviathan is a monstrous fish created on the fifth day of Creation. Its story is recounted in the Talmud (*Baba Bathra* 74b), where it is told that the Leviathan will be slain, its flesh will be served as a feast to the righteous at the End of Days (Messianic Age), and its skin will be used to cover the tent where the banquet will take place.

351 *Tausves-Yontof*: Heine's transcription of an Ashkenazic pronunciation of the *Tosafot Yomtov*, a commentary on the Talmud by the major scholar Rabbi Yom Tov Lipmann Heller (1579–1654). Ashkenazic Jews are the Jews of Germany, France, and Eastern Europe.

371 *Korah*: Leader of a rebellion against Moses and his brother Aaron during the journey of the Israelites from Egypt to the land of Israel. As punishment, he was swallowed up by the earth.

384 *Sodomites*: Residents of the biblical city of Sodom who were destroyed by God as a punishment for their wickedness.

402–3 *Lucifer and Beelzebub . . . Belial and Ashtoreth*: The ruler of hell is Lucifer and Beelzebub, Belial, and Ashtoreth are hell's princes. The names Beelzebub, Belial, and Ashtoreth are derived from pagan idols. —J. P.

DIMYONOT דמיונות
Jews and the Cultural Imagination

Samantha Baskind, General Editor

Volumes in the Dimyonot series explore the intersections, and interstices, of Jewish experience and culture. These projects emerge from many disciplines—including art, history, language, literature, music, religion, philosophy, and cultural studies—and diverse chronological and geographical locations. Each volume, however, interrogates the multiple and evolving representations of Judaism and Jewishness, by both Jews and non-Jews, over time and place.